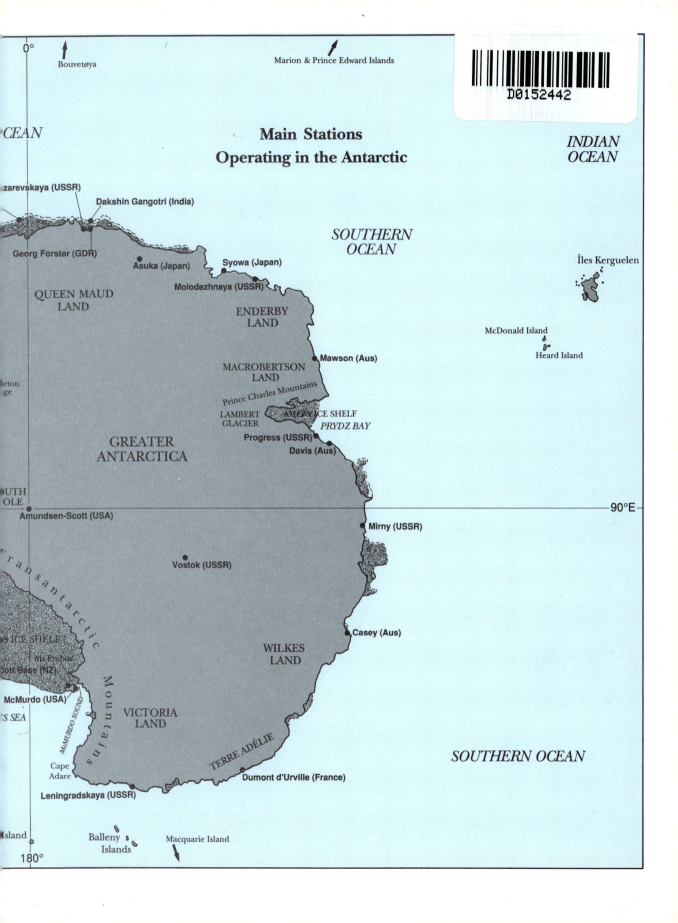

Main Stations
Operating in the Antarctic

0°

Bouvetøya

Marion & Prince Edward Islands

CEAN

INDIAN OCEAN

zarevskaya (USSR)

Dakshin Gangotri (India)

Georg Forster (GDR)

SOUTHERN OCEAN

Îles Kerguelen

Asuka (Japan)

Syowa (Japan)

Molodezhnaya (USSR)

QUEEN MAUD LAND

ENDERBY LAND

McDonald Island

Heard Island

Mawson (Aus)

MACROBERTSON LAND

leton
ge

Prince Charles Mountains

AMERY ICE SHELF

LAMBERT GLACIER

PRYDZ BAY

GREATER ANTARCTICA

Progress (USSR)

Davis (Aus)

UTH
OLE

90°E

Amundsen-Scott (USA)

Mirny (USSR)

Vostok (USSR)

ransantarctic

Casey (Aus)

WILKES LAND

ICE SHELF

Mt. Erebus

olt Base (NZ)

McMurdo (USA)

S SEA

Mountains

McMURDO SOUND

VICTORIA LAND

Cape Adare

TERRE ADÉLIE

SOUTHERN OCEAN

Dumont d'Urville (France)

Leningradskaya (USSR)

sland

Balleny Islands

Macquarie Island

180°

ANTARCTICA
THE LAST FRONTIER

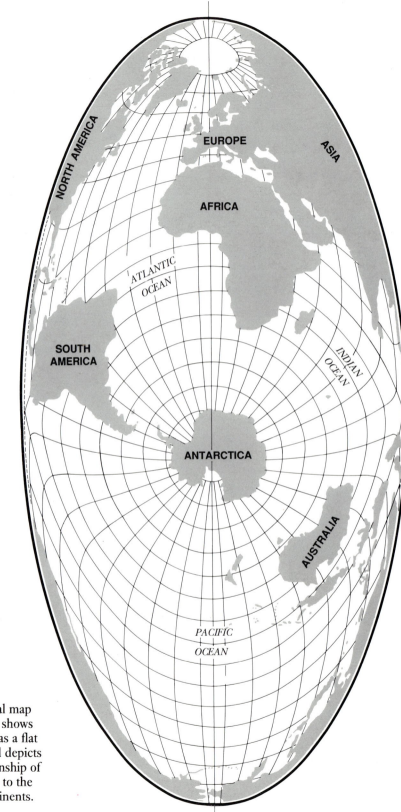

An unusual map projection shows the Earth as a flat ellipse and depicts the relationship of Antarctica to the other continents.

Richard Laws

ANTARCTICA

THE LAST FRONTIER

ANGLIA
Television Limited

Boxtree

First published in 1989 by Boxtree Limited

Front jacket photograph: Survival Anglia/Joel Bennett
Back jacket photographs: Survival Anglia/Rick Price

The publishers and author wish to thank the following sources for use of photographs on the pages listed:
Survival Anglia/Rick Price 17, 21, 40, 41, 54, 55, 65, 73, 76, 77, 78, 79, 80, 82, 83, 86, 93, 94, 100, 101, 104, 108, 109, 121, 122, 124, 125, 126, 127, 132, 133, 134, 137, 138, 140, 142, 144, 145, 154, 155, 156, 157, 169, 170, 173, 198, 200, 204.
Survival Anglia/Annie Price 110, 114, 115, 186.
Survival Anglia/Joel Bennett 111, 202.
Bernard Moran and the following British Antarctic Survey photographers:
C.J. Gilbert 12, 13, 14, 50, 51 , 102, 103, 123 D. Walton 20 C. Swithinbank 24, 25 R.I.L. Smith 33, 34, 35, 49, 171 C. Ellis-Evans 52, 53 D. Allan 56, 57, 67, 68, 72, 74, 75, 81. Ric Jordan 87, 88 D. Wynne-Williams 27 N. Leader-Williams 183 I. Hawes 68, 69 B. Storey 158, 159 M. Thomson 185 G. Renner 165 D.R. Cripps 130, 131 I.L. Boyd 146 I. Everson 92, 93, 95 P. Rodhouse 96, 98, 99 D.R.W. Block 64, 66 D. Morris 90.

Sea Mammal Research Unit and A.R. Martin 148, 149

T.G. Smith 152

Satellite Mosaic courtesy of NOAA NRSC (pages 10-11)
Satellite images courtesy of NASA (pages 33, 34, 35, 192)

British Library Cataloguing in Publication Data
Laws, R.M. (Richard Maitland)
    Antarctica.
    1. Antartica. Natural environment
    I. Title
    508.98'9

    ISBN 1-85283-247-9

Edited by Christopher Stocks
Designed by Groom and Pickerill

Typeset by York House Typographic
Printed and bound in Italy by OFSA S.p.A
For Boxtree Limited, 36 Tavistock Street,
London. WC2E 7PB.

Contents

Foreword by Lord Buxton

It gives me tremendous pleasure to introduce *Antarctica: The Last Frontier*, especially when the author Richard Laws is a leading authority on the Antarctic, and an old friend.

The publication of this book is well-timed, not only as a contribution to the current political debate on the continuance of the Antarctic Treaty but also, more widely, in the light of growing public concern about the long-term consequences of environmental pollution. The Antarctic represents an international challenge, a chance to manage a continent that is as yet virtually unspoiled by human activities. Will we continue in our old ways and exploit the delicate natural systems beyond repair, or will we learn from our past mistakes and work together to respect and conserve something for the future?

Anglia Television has produced several programmes over the last thirty years down south in the Antarctic, the Falklands and South Georgia. But Anglia's latest television series, produced with its acclaimed 'Survival' team, is the first to present a comprehensive picture of the political dilemma over Antarctica's future. It could never have been achieved without the formidable partnership of the British Antarctic Survey, which was the key to the entire venture. This book is the mirror and the counterpart of the television series.

Through BAS, the United Kingdom leads the rest of the world in the Antarctic. For many years BAS's pioneering role was not appreciated in Whitehall and one or two of us fought lonely battles to save the organisation from being run down. However, in 1982 the opportunity arose to explain the situation personally to the Prime Minister and from then on everything was put right. BAS has since alerted the world to the damage we are inflicting on the upper atmosphere.

Dick Laws was director of BAS for many years and remains a leading light in Antarctic research and policy-making. Paradoxically we first met nearly thirty years ago in the heart of Africa. He is not only a fine writer and photographer; few people know that he is also a talented wildlife and landscape painter. It is most fortunate that with this book he has made a vital contribution to the public knowledge of the Antarctic and its crucial role in the future of our planet.

Aubrey Buxton.

INTRODUCTION

In 1947, at the age of 21 and newly graduated from university, I had the privilege of sailing to the Antarctic in a small wooden ship, the M/V John Biscoe — a voyage that took six weeks and was an adventure in itself. Before that time my knowledge of Antarctica was virtually confined to the classics of exploration I had read as a boy.

For two years I was in charge of a small base on Signy Island in the South Orkneys, where I studied the biology of the elephant seal, returning for a further year on South Georgia. Later I spent seven months as a Government Whaling Inspector and biologist on a whaling factory ship. Those seven months were spent almost entirely out of sight of land.

In later years I studied the biology of Antarctic whales, and, after a period in East Africa, spent a series of summer trips on continental Antarctica, the Antarctic Peninsula and amongst the offshore islands. Altogether I must have spent at least half my life in Antarctic work and some six full years living there. The latter part was spent as Director of the British Antarctic Survey, which is internationally acknowledged as the leading Antarctic research organisation. I am a committed Antarctican.

Little is known about Antarctica by the general public and, considering its influence on the global environment, this is a cause for concern. So when, in 1985, Aubrey Buxton, Chairman of Anglia Television, came up with the idea of making a series of television programmes about the Antarctic I was enthusiastic, and offered the resources of the British Antarctic Survey. Some former members of the BAS have been involved in the series as cameramen (Doug Allan and Rick Price), and I was able to see another Anglia team (Joel Bennett and Luisa Stoughton) in action in the field.

The story begins with the creation of the Antarctic environment. First there were the very large-scale processes of plate tectonics and continental drift that led to the break-up of the original southern supercontinent, Gondwana, processes that left Antarctica and its offshore islands occupying the positions they do today.

In the past, Antarctica had a warm climate, supporting luxuriant vegetation and large animals, but as the climate deteriorated over the last thirty million years this flora and fauna disappeared. Despite the broad barrier of the Southern Ocean and the continuing cold, however, life still retains a tenuous foothold there.

Nearly half of Antarctica's coastline is hidden by thick floating ice shelves or glaciers, and the rest is scoured down to a depth of fifteen metres or more by icebergs, which limits coastal life. But below the level of the sea ice, where water temperatures are stable, there is a colourful marine world containing a great diversity of life.

The Southern Ocean makes up one tenth of the world ocean, and the expansion and contraction of its sea ice is the largest seasonal process on Earth. Recent work has revealed that pack ice provides a surprisingly productive winter habitat for a number of small creatures, the most important of them being the krill.

Krill, which looks like a little shrimp, probably has a total weight in excess of any other animal in the world, including the human race. Krill is the staple food of the oceanic squids and of most Antarctic fishes, birds, seals and whales. Only in the last few years has its struggle to survive become apparent: if it doesn't find enough food, or if the oxygen in the water decreases slightly, it plunges under its own weight to depths where it dies from oxygen starvation.

Dependent on krill are the seabirds and the seals. Like the Antarctic squids and fishes they are represented by few species, but each species contains huge numbers of individuals. Also feeding on the krill are the baleen whales whose overall numbers are probably larger than ever before, despite the huge reductions in numbers of some species by the whaling industry.

Finally there is the human race, which did not arrive on the scene until the last century. We have had many adverse impacts on Antarctica, directly in the case of fishing (for seals, whales, fish and now even krill and squids), and indirectly through the introduction of cats, rats and reindeer. The burning of fossil fuels and the destruction of the forests has increased the carbon dioxide level in the atmosphere, leading to the 'greenhouse effect'. This is predicted to warm our planet by as much as $7°C$ at the poles, with devastating implications for the Antarctic ice cap and its pack ice, not to mention global sea-levels.

Furthermore, all life on earth is protected from lethal ultraviolet radiation from the sun by a thin layer of ozone in the upper atmosphere. It was research in the Antarctic which gave the first indication that man-made chemicals — the chlorofluorocarbons, or CFCs, used in foams, aerosols, refrigerators and air conditioners — were drastically thinning the ozone layer. As Mustafa Tolba, Director of the United Nations Environment Programme, has said, 'Today one fact of human life is more certain than ever: that the stakes involved in finding solutions to man-made environmental problems are no less than the future and fate of our planet.'

Antarctica holds important keys to the solution of these problems; for example, the archive of climate and pollution that lies locked in the Antarctic ice cap, which can also serve as a baseline against which to measure global increases in pollutants. Antarctic research can also help predict the potential changes in future world sea levels. On a physical level, the vast expanses of the Southern Ocean provide an important 'sink' for carbon dioxide, thus counteracting the greenhouse effect.

It is fortunate, then, that the Antarctic is an area of unrivalled international cooperation under the umbrella of the Antarctic Treaty. To date 38 nations have signed the Treaty, representing 80 per cent of mankind, and other important international agreements have been negotiated by the Treaty nations. These agreements, known collectively as the Antarctic Treaty System, demonstrate great foresight because they have all been signed in advance of actual practical problems.

The intention of this book is to bring to as wide a public as possible the uniqueness and importance of the Antarctic, both in its resources and the key role it can play in helping to avert environmental disaster on our planet. In attempting to achieve this aim I have been helped by many people. First I wish to acknowledge the sustained support of Aubrey Buxton in my years as Director of the British Antarctic Survey, often at times of great political and actual pressure (such as the Falklands War), as well as for his suggestion that I write this book. Jeremy Bradshaw, Graham Creelman and David Hickman of Anglia Television have also been most helpful and supportive throughout the venture. It has also been my pleasure to plan and work with Sarah Mahaffy and Janita Clamp of Boxtree. I hope the book meets up to their expectations.

I would like to take this opportunity to acknowledge the help of all those who have contributed to my knowledge of Antarctica, for this is a very wide field, beyond the comprehension of one person. I should start with the late Brian Roberts (Head of the Polar Regions Section at the Foreign and Commonwealth Office), who recruited me to Antarctic research, as well as Derek Maling and the late Ralph Lenton, who shared those early years at Signy.

Foremost among the others, either through their writings, in discussion, or for other help are my friends and colleagues in BAS and in the international community, through the Scientific Committee on Antarctic Research. It is invidious to mention names but some naturally come forward: J. Bawden, J. Bengtson, G.C.L. Bertram, W. Block, W.N. Bonner, A. Clarke, J.P. Croxall, D.J. Drewry, J.R. Dudeney, S.Z. El-Sayed, I. Everson, G.E. Fogg, V.E. Fuchs, M. Hallatt, R.B. Heywood, G.A. Knox, G.A. Llano, C. Lorius, T. Nemoto, J. Priddle, G. de Q. Robin, M.J. Rycroft, D.B. Siniff, R.I.L. Smith, C.W.M. Swithinbank, M.R.A. Thomson, G.E. Todd and D.W.H. Walton.

All these and more have contributed to my achievements, my education and my thinking about Antarctica, but I alone bear responsibility for the views advanced in this book and for any factual errors it may contain.

Finally I would like to thank my family for putting up with my frequent lengthy absences in the field and at conferences, to my youngest son Andrew for his patience in explaining to me the mysterious workings of my word processor, and especially to my wife Maureen for loyal and loving support over the years, when in the struggles with central bureaucracy the way has often been rather rough.

Richard Laws
St Edmund's College
Cambridge
28th February 1989

ANTARCTIC LANDS

Antarctica – a composite picture derived from satellite imagery. It shows clearly Greater and Lesser Antarctica divided by the Transantarctic Mountains, the projection of the Antarctic Peninsula, and the large embayments of the Ross and Weddell Seas.

The past: drifting continents

The breakup of Gondwana. Distribution of land: (a) 200 million years ago, (b) 60 million years ago (c) at present. There is still uncertainty about the earlier position of the Antarctic Peninsula (red).

Hidden deep beneath the icy dome of the Antarctic is the world's fifth largest continent. Covering 14 million square kilometres it is twice as big as Australia, and nearly sixty times the size of Britain. One hundred and eighty million years ago this continent was the keystone of a great southern supercontinent called Gondwana. Then it began to break up, with the separation first of what is now South America and Africa and then India and Australia. Later, around 135 million years ago, Africa and South America themselves began to drift apart. By 55 million years ago Australia had separated from Antarctica, and the continent was finally isolated, some 28 million years ago, with the severing of the Antarctic Peninsula from the tip of South America.

The theory of continental drift was first proposed by the German meteorologist Alfred Wegener, but despite the solid geological evidence published in 1937 by the geologist Alexander du Toit, the theory remained extremely controversial for a further 25 years, since there was no apparent mechanism that could actually cause continents to drift around the world.

But the theory of plate tectonics, which was developed during the 1960s,

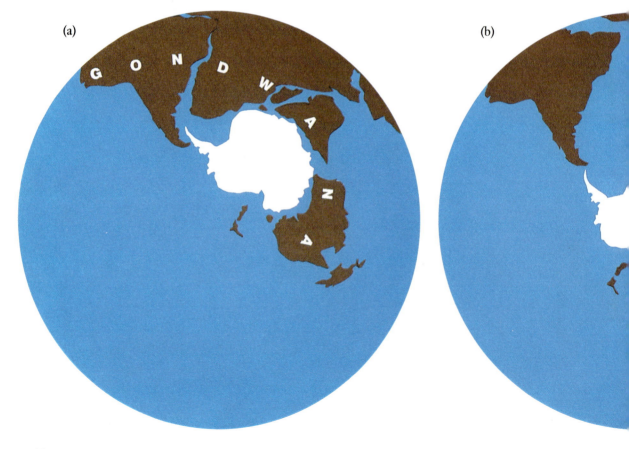

(a)

(b)

came up with convincing arguments to suggest that the surface of the Earth supports six solid 'plates', which float, as it were, on the more molten material underneath. Not only does this theory explain the locations of earthquake zones and volcanoes (which coincide with the grating boundaries between two plates) but also the phenomenon of mid-oceanic ridges, which form where two plates are moving apart, allowing molten rock to well up from beneath. This is known as sea-floor spreading.

Gradually this theory has allowed us to piece together the evolution of the Antarctic archipelago, the history of its climate and the circumpolar ocean currents which led to the formation of the present ice cap. By eighty million years ago there was already a long, shallow seaway between Antarctica and Australia, but deep water did not begin to flow until 25 to 30 million years ago, while the initial opening of the Drake Passage between Antarctica and South America occurred only 28 million years ago. Even before this, however, the area now occupied by the subglacial basins in Lesser Antarctica would have constituted a shallow sea in the ice-free period before the creation of the Drake Passage. But with the development of the deep Antarctic Circumpolar Current around 28 million years ago the continent was cut off from the warmer oceans of the world, and its frozen days began.

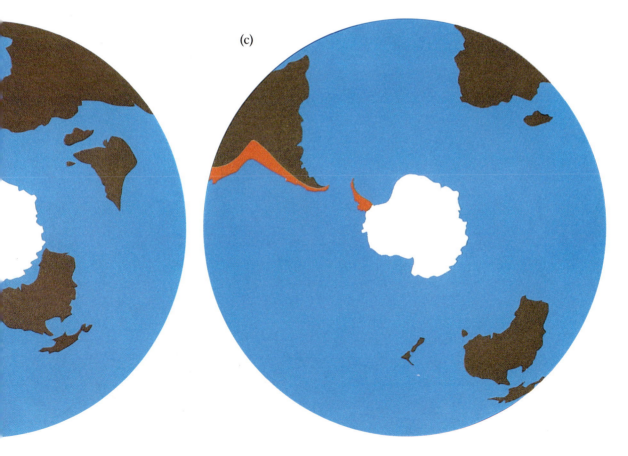

(c)

opposite
LANDSAT satellite picture showing Rutford Ice Stream flowing between Fletcher Promontory (above) and the highest mountain range in Antarctica, the Ellsworth Mountains (below). The ice surface reflects the sub-glacial topography.

below
Section through the Antarctic ice sheet from Ronne Entrance (75°W), south of Alexander Island, Bellingshausen Sea, Lesser Antarctica to Colvocoresses Bay (114°E), Greater Antarctica.

The present: bedrock and ice cover

The geology of Antarctica has never been investigated in the kind of detail accorded to other continents, for the simple reason that only about two per cent of its surface is clear of a thick coating of permanent ice. Only during the last thirty years have remote-sensing techniques of geophysical exploration such as seismic and radio-echo soundings been able to give us a picture of the continent which lies beneath the ice.

Geologically, the Antarctic can be divided into two parts, divided by the Transantarctic Mountains, which extend for some 3,500 kilometres and whose peaks, for the most part, protrude above the surface of the ice. The larger region, Greater (or East) Antarctica is an ancient block or shield composed of rocks as much as 3,800 million years old, and mostly above sea level.

In complete contrast, the bedrock underlying much of Lesser, or West, Antarctica dates from a mere 150 to 200 million years ago. Lesser Antarctica also has ranges of mountains which are Himalayan in scale, but the weight of the ice pushes much of this half of the continent down as far as 2,500 metres beneath the surface of the sea. Mountain chains lie along its Pacific coast and the Antarctic Pensinsula; inland, the Ellsworth Mountains include the highest peak in Antarctica, the Vinson Massif, which rises to 5,140 metres above sea level. Computer analysis suggests that if the ice sheet was ever removed the centre of Greater Antarctica would rise by 1,000 metres and Lesser Antarctica by 500 metres. At the same time the water produced by the melting ice would raise the level of the Earth's oceans by nearly sixty metres, flooding vast areas of the Earth.

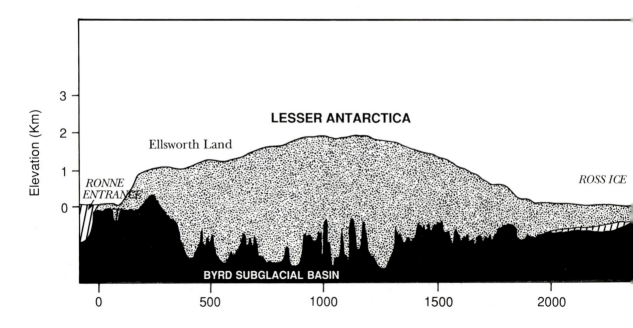

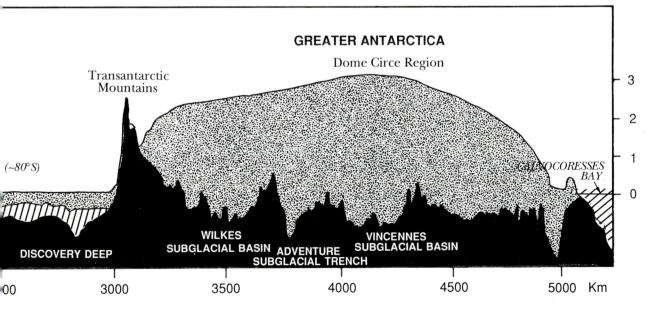

Fossils

above
A fossil ammonite, from Alexander Island.

below
A frond of a tree fern, a fossil from Alexander Island clearly indicating a much warmer climate 100 million years ago.

Again, because so little of Antarctica's surface is exposed, our record of its fossils is fragmentary compared with that of more accessible regions of the world. However, the marine sediments of the Antarctic Pensinsula yield an abundant and varied selection of fossil forms. For example between 30 and 60 million years ago ammonites, gastropods, nautiloids, belemnites, crinoids, asteroids, ophiuroids, brachiopods, bryozoans, annelids and crustacea. From 65 million years ago come fish, sharks teeth, turtles, whales, an extinct marsupial called Polydops (previously only known from Patagonia), and four types of fossil penguins, including a giant standing 1.35 metres tall.

Plant fossils are found in rocks from about 250 million years ago when the climate improved after an earlier glaciation; they include the fern-like Pteridophytes, conifers and Cycads like palm trees. Even fossil pollens have been discovered, including those of trees similar to the southern beech (which still grow in the forests of Tasmania and Tierra del Fuego), and of the so-called monkey-puzzle tree, which was typical of the cool, temperate climate of the Antarctic about 50 million years ago.

1 cm

Ice

The expansion of the Southern Ocean by sea-floor spreading and the establishment of the Antarctic Circumpolar Current created a physical barrier between Antarctica and the warmer waters and lands to the north. More than anything else it was this barrier which led to the progressive refrigeration of the Antarctic and the concomitant growth of the ice sheet.

Antarctica is high and cold and dry, the reverse of the Arctic, where a deep ocean basin is surrounded for the most part by low-lying land. Antarctica is, in fact, the highest continent on earth, three times the average height of any other. It is also by far the coldest continent, with a mean annual temperature at the South Pole of -49°C. At Vostok Station, which stands 3,488 metres above sea level on ice 3.7 kilometres thick, the annual mean is -55°C. Here also has been recorded the lowest temperature on earth: -89°C. Such extreme temperatures are a result not just of Antarctica's isolation, but also because, with the Earth tilting on its axis, the sun is below

Snow drifting in winter over consolidated pack ice.

the horizon for nearly six months of the year. Worse still, what little sunlight the continent does receive is largely reflected by the ice. This means, that Antarctica actually loses more heat every year than it gains, an effect intensified by the fact that sea ice, with its similarly high reflectivity, almost doubles the size of the continent by the end of every winter.

Taken as a whole, the ice-covered area of Antarctica represents nearly a tenth of the Earth's surface, and is the point where most of the world's heat-loss takes place. This is extremely important to the global climate, because the great temperature difference between the tropics and the poles leads to enormous transfers of energy, which in turn drive the Earth's weather system.

Aerial view of a nunatak in Southern Palmer Land, Antarctic Peninsula. The North-facing slopes are relatively free of snow and ice.

The Antarctic, then, is the most glaciated continent in the world, containing 90 per cent of the world's ice and nearly three quarters of its fresh water. This vast ice sheet is fed by an annual accumulation of only five centimetres of snow near the South Pole, increasing to 50 to a 100 centimetres near the coast. Snowfall is notoriously difficult to record, but there are estimates of the total balance. Over the major part of Greater Antarctica the annual snowfall is thought to be less than ten grammes per square centimetre, and over a smaller area (though this still comprises some two million square kilometres) less than five. This makes Antarctica one of the most arid deserts on earth.

It is so cold here that the snow which falls on the polar plateau rarely melts. Instead it accumulates in a dense consolidated mass called firn, which then turns into ice. In its turn this ice is compacted, and flows down towards the coastal ice shelves. At the same time these fringing ice shelves are being broken up by ocean currents, tides and waves; even on occasion by tsunami (tidal waves). This produces icebergs, some of which may be 240 kilometres long and 110 kilometres wide, large enough to be tracked by satellites for several years before they melt. It is interesting to note that the latest estimates of the annual iceberg production, although subject to considerable uncertainties, are quite close to the most recent estimates of Antarctica's annual accumulation of snow. These very approximate estimates suggest that the ice volume is either very near to a stable balance, or possibly slowly declining.

Evening light over Laws Glacier, Coronation Island, South Orkney Islands.

19

The present weather and climate

Until the first permanent research stations were established between thirty and forty years ago, our knowledge of the Antarctic climate was very patchy: even the longest run of climatic data goes back only as far as 1903.

The climate and weather of Antarctica is dominated by three factors: the waters of the Southern Ocean, the seasonal variations in the sea ice cover, and the continental ice sheet. There are pronounced climatic differences between the continental interior, the coastal margins and the Southern Ocean itself, which tends to be much cloudier than Lesser Antarctica, which itself is more cloudy than Greater Antarctica, with its arid high plateau.

Surface temperatures depend primarily on height, but the mean annual temperature also decreases with increasing latitudes. At sub-Antarctic islands summer temperatures may be 12-14°C. Even on the continental coasts (up to about 70 degrees south) the maximum summer temperature can be more than nine degrees centigrade. On the South Orkneys the minimum temperature falls to -40°C in midwinter (August) and I have experienced temperatures of -35°C camping out in June. At higher latitudes much lower temperatures are common, down to -56.7°C, for example, in the Ellsworth Range. One of the most distinctive features of this climate is the formation of surface layers of exceptionally cold air, which produce striking mirages.

opposite
A large crevasse, about 40 metres deep, in the Nye Glacier, Antarctic Peninsula.

below
Weathered bergy-bit frozen into the sea ice.

Brandy Bay, James Ross Island, near the tip of the Antarctic Peninsula. The prominent rock outcrops are volcanic plugs. This island has thick sedimentary rock layers and if commercial exploratory drilling for oil or gas occurs it will be a likely location.

Wind speeds on the high polar plateau, where temperatures are low, also tend to be low, but by contrast at Cape Denison on the coast the mean wind speed over a period of four years was 67 kilometres an hour — by far the highest wind speed near sea level anywhere on Earth. Observations taken from ships show that wind speeds drop dramatically only a few kilometres away from the coast, but when climatic depressions pass wind speeds of up to 180 kilometres an hour or more are not uncommon.

The final climatic peculiarities of the Antarctic are the regions known as oases. These areas, first described on Alexander Island, are characterised by the amount of bare ground they display, the rock and soil of which absorbs more solar radiation in summer, making them warmer than their surroundings. In winter, however, long-wave radiation from the bare ground leads to lower temperatures in oases than those in the ice-covered areas around them. Wind speeds also tend to be lower in oases than elsewhere.

Soils

The physical and chemical processes which produce soil in the Antarctic are identical to those which occur in the temperate regions of the world, but the rates at which they proceed are much slower because of Antarctica's sub-zero temperatures and the fact that nearly all of its water is locked in ice. In some extreme cases, therefore, soil formation can be measured, not in hundreds, but in millions of years: one dry valley soil has been given an age of 4.1 million years.

Soils can be classified in various ways. One approach is to describe them in terms of their composition. Ahumic soil, as its name suggests, contains no humus and very little living matter, whereas ornithogenic soil is derived from the excreta from bird colonies and is often rich in living organisms.

An alternative approach is to classify soils in regional terms. Three main Antarctic soil zones have been recognised. First comes the zone associated with the Transantarctic Mountains, which have arguably the most hostile environment on Earth. Many hundreds of square kilometres of ahumic soils in the dry valleys of South Victoria Land are apparently totally barren and have been studied by the United States Government Space Agency, NASA, for their resemblance to the soils of Mars: the 'Viking' Mars probe was tested here.

The coastal regions of Greater Antarctica form the second major soil zone. Here the temperature is much warmer and the soil temperatures, to a depth of one metre, may be as high as 4°C. As a result of these higher temperatures there is more free water and weathering is greater and deeper. The soils of this zone are more organic than those of the Transantarctic mountains, although they are still relatively dry, and mosses and lichens are more abundant, particularly on sheltered, north-facing slopes.

The third soil zone belongs to the maritime Antarctic, the West coast of the Antarctic peninsula, its islands and the South Atlantic islands. Here the climate is less extreme, with smaller daily fluctuations and frequent drizzle (and even drenching rain) in summer. The air temperature may be at 0°C at any time of the year, but rises to 10°C in the warmest months, January and February. Under these cool oceanic conditions soil formation is more rapid than on the continent, and soils are subjected to high moisture levels and regular cycles of freezing and thawing. Where the surface is unstable due to such processes the soil may be very young, although the abundant moisture and higher temperatures promote chemical weathering. Such soils may have quantities of carbon and nitrogen, particularly in the vicinity of bird or seal colonies.

In the northern, sub-Antarctic parts of this region, there is a much wider range of soil types than in the other two zones, and these in their turn support a much wider range of vegetation. In South Georgia, for example, there are organic soils, meadow tundra soils, brown soils, mineral soils and peat deposits that have increased at a constant rate for ten thousand years.

Cliffs of shelf ice
showing
accumulation of
annual layers.

Inland waters

In the icy continent of Antarctica liquid water is generally restricted to the
warmer areas of the coasts and offshore islands. At higher latitudes there are
some salt water lakes, and even stratified lakes, where fresh water lies on top
of salt water. In these cold climates the upper layers of many lakes are frozen
for up to ten months of the year, during which time the liquid water beneath
effectively becomes a closed system. The lake's icy surface is covered with
more and more snow, which protects it from the worst extremes of the
climate in the air above, allowing the winter survival of living organisms.

However, because of snow's high reflectivity (also referred to as its albedo) little of the sunlight which is essential to life passes through the snow and ice layers to the underlying water. In some situations vertical clear columnar crystals of ice may form in the surface layer, which act as light-conductors, increasing the penetration of sunlight into the water.

An evolutionary pattern has been proposed which relates the stage of a lake's development to the time elapsed since the retreat of overlying ice. As the area around the lake is exposed and develops plant life, so the nutrient content of the lake increases. Lakes near the sea are further influenced by wind-blown spray and by seal or bird colonies, paralleling the evolution of soils described in the previous section. There are some nutrients even in apparently pristine snow, introduced by windblown dust, whose presence is revealed by the development of green or pink tinges caused by the growth of algae.

In the first stages of lake formation, melt-water pools may develop in the ice. This is especially noticeable in certain areas of George VI Sound, where shallow pools are so common at the height of summer that they hinder surface travel. But this is a seasonal phenomenon: their lifespan is short and they freeze solid again in winter.

The next step in the evolution of Antarctic lakes are what are called proglacial lakes. These are formed when a rock basin or moraine becomes dammed by a barrier of ice. Again, they often fluctuate in size on a seasonal basis, or over the years, as the ice dam gradually melts.

Freshwater lakes at Maiviken, Cumberland Bay, South Georgia, surrounded by tussock grass.

When the ice recedes still further more permanent lake basins are exposed, and as the surrounding soils and vegetation evolve, the lake slowly comes to hold more nutrients, although still at relatively low levels (unless, again, it is naturally enriched by seal faeces or penguin guano).

Finally there is the special category of saline lakes, which can arise in two different ways. Some originate when sea water is trapped in bays or fjords after the sea has flooded the land and subsequently retreated. The other type is found in areas like the dry valleys of South Victoria Land, where evaporation exceeds precipitation, leading eventually to lakes whose water can be 13 times more salty than sea water. If fresh melt-water then enters the lake it does not mix with the denser salty water, but instead lies over it and forms a stratified lake.

Canopus Pond, a hypersaline stratified lake in Wright Valley, dry valleys, Victoria Land. This is one of the most nearly sterile areas on the Earth.

27

Such stratified lakes can also form, however, where a thick floating ice shelf meets the land, holding back a depth of anything up to 200 metres of melt-water, but also allowing communication with the open sea under the ice shelf at a deeper level. Thus these lakes may be tidal, even at a great distance from the open sea, and can unexpectedly contain both fresh-water and marine life. One example is Ablation Lake in Alexander Island.

Aerial view of Ablation Lake, a stratified tidal lake on Alexander Island; the smooth ice-covered lake is hemmed in by pressure ridges of George VI Ice Shelf.

In the more extreme environment of continental Antarctica the great salinity of some water reduces its freezing point so far that such lakes may remain unfrozen at temperatures as low as -55°C. Surface ice does not form and so they are not insulated from the winter climate, and so they rarely support life: in fact they may even be virtually sterile.

THE SOUTHERN OCEAN

Small tabular
iceberg in the
Weddell Sea;
evening light.

Great waters

The vast Southern Ocean encircles the Antarctic in a continuous ring of mainly eastward-flowing water, connecting the three oceans to the north. This also isolates Antarctica from their warmer waters. This Antarctic Circumpolar Current is the only true global current, endlessly circling around 24,000 kilometres and ranging from 200 to 1,000 kilometres wide. Enormous quantities of water flow through it (on average 130 million cubic metres every second), although there are large differences from year to year and even week to week. The average rate of flow of this current exceeds that

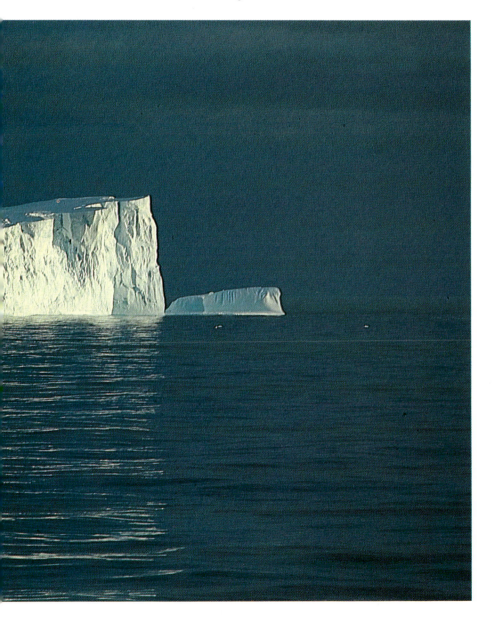

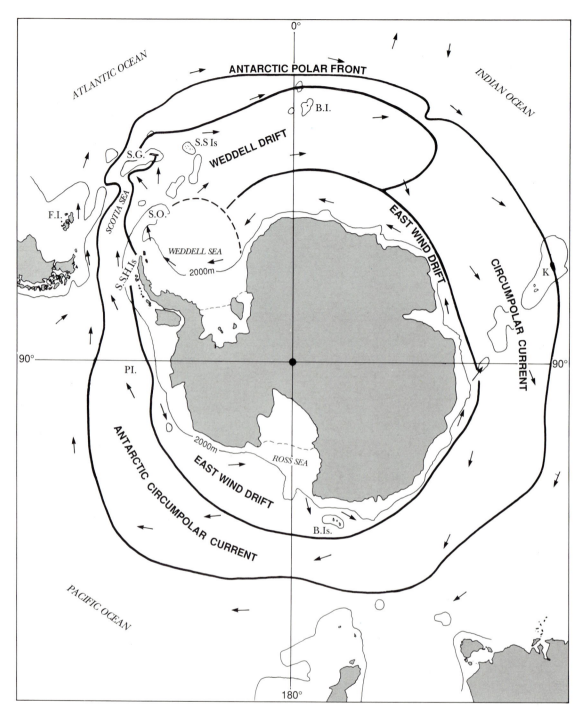

of the Gulf Stream by four times, and the Mississippi River by 400 times. The Antarctic Circumpolar current is driven by strong winds from the West; nearer the continent easterly winds maintain the shallower smaller-scale East Wind Drift.

An important feature of the Southern Ocean is the Antarctic Polar Front. This is the zone where the cold surface waters of the Antarctic (which are near freezing point even in summer) meet the warmer, southward-flowing waters from the Atlantic, Pacific and Indian Oceans. The seas south of the Polar Front extend over 35 million square kilometres and make up a tenth of all the world's oceans. They also contain the coldest and densest water on earth, the Antarctic Bottom Water. As this cold water sinks it flows over the world's ocean floors and reduces the temperature of more than half the world's seas to less than 2°C. This is one of the major ways in which it affects the climate of the earth, counterbalancing the effect of the tropics. Cold Antarctic water is also full of oxygen, and it aerates the world's oceans.

Opposite
Approximate boundaries of Antarctic water masses at the surface and directions of the main surface currents.

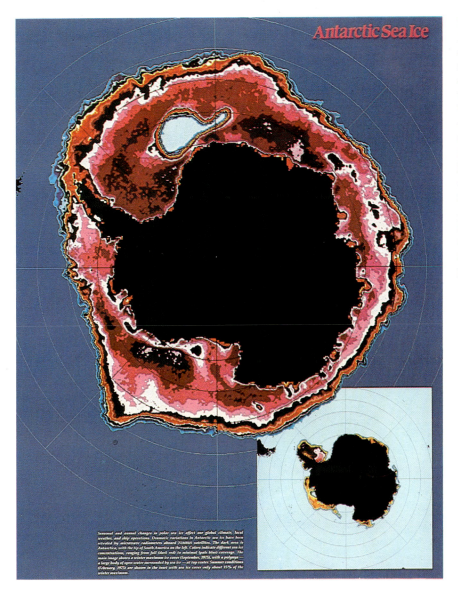

Antarctic Sea Ice

Satellite image of Antarctica (black) during winter 1974, showing the extent of sea ice (reds) and the very large Weddell polyna which formed in the winters of 1974, 1975 and 1976 but has not been seen since. At its largest it measured 300,000 square kilometres. Inset: residual pack ice regions in the previous summer.

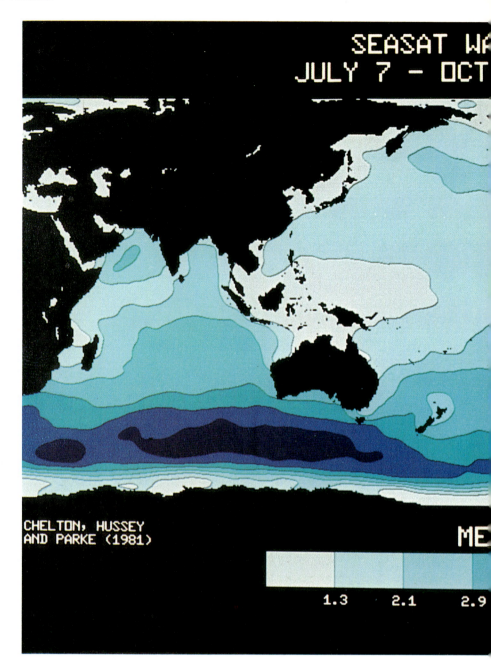

Average wave heights obtained from satellite altimetry; circumpolar winds sweeping the Southern Ocean create the world's stormiest seas.

The Southern Ocean is not contained within the circle formed by the Antarctic Polar Front, but its northern boundary remains undefined. Within this area, complicated wind and oceanographic conditions cause water carried by the Antarctic Circumpolar Current to move vertically upwards to the surface at around one third of the horizontal rate of flow. Cold, relatively fresh surface water is continually replaced by the Circumpolar Deep Water, two to three degrees warmer and more salty. This 'upwelling' at the

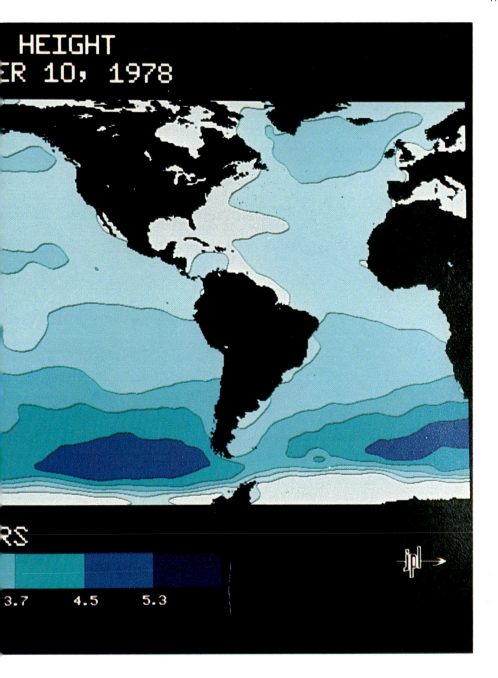

Antarctic Divergence is an important oceanic process because it brings nutrients to the surface. There the upwelled water remains for an average of two years, while its nutrients are taken up by microscopic phytoplankton.

The Antarctic seas are a mixture of waters which can be traced to their origins by their temperature and the balance of salts they carry: some highly saline waters have even been traced back to the Mediterranean. However, the Southern Ocean is so dense that the generally lighter waters from the north have to rise very dramatically, by oceanographic standards, to override them. Between the north and south sides of the Drake Passage, for example, the depth of water at 1°C rises from 3,500 to 1,000 metres, which constitutes a slope of 1:720.

South of the Polar Front there is, for much of the year, a layer of relatively fresh water, roughly 100 metres deep, just below the surface, created by the melting of the pack ice. As this cold, fresh, well-oxygenated 'winter water' layer moves away from the continent it gradually sinks, and slowly spreads throughout the oceans of the southern hemisphere.

Coastal polyna off low ice cliffs of the Filchner Ice Shelf, Weddell Sea. The smooth water surface is due to frazil ice and pancake ice is forming in the foreground.

Sea ice

The ice we have examined so far has mainly been produced by snow falling over the land, which is then compressed, flows and enters the seas over the continental shelves. In the Antarctic, however, most life is found not on land but in the seas, and the type of ice which most directly affects it is also formed in the sea. This ice is called fast ice and pack ice, and it freezes and melts each year, expanding to form an area of as much as 20 million square kilometres every winter. But by the end of the summer (December

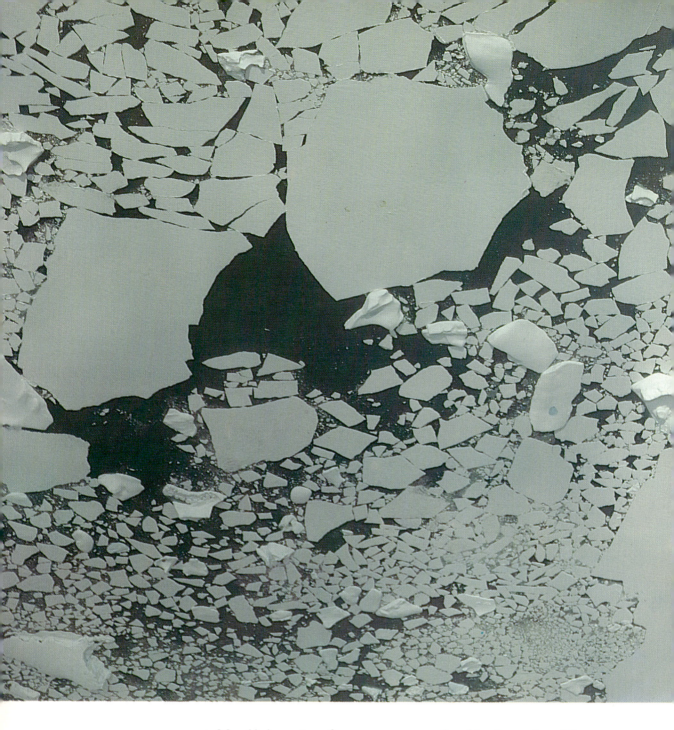

to March) the action of waves, currents and melting has reduced that area to only 4 million square kilometres.

This is the largest seasonal process in the Earth's oceans and it effectively doubles the area of the Antarctic ice blanket from 18 to 34 million square kilometres. It has a huge effect on world climate by increasing the amount of reflection of incoming radiant energy from the sun and reducing its

Aerial view of fast ice breaking up in Marguerite Bay, Antarctic Peninsula to form small floes.

penetration into the sea. The rate of build-up of sea ice in autumn and winter (February to September) is much slower than the rate of decay (October to January), and it seems possible that the layers of pigmented algae found in sea ice may, by absorbing solar radiation in summer, accelerate its disappearance. If so it is a remarkable example of the influence of a microscopic life form on the world's climate.

Sea ice formation and chemistry

Sea ice may be formed in three ways, 'Frazil ice' consists of small ice crystals (about one millimetre long) which often form under stormy conditions, quickly coagulating into small sugary-looking floes often with turned-up edges caused by their bumping together (these floes are called 'pancake ice'). 'Congelation ice' is formed slowly by heat loss underneath an overlying layer of ice. The larger crystals have a columnar structure which subsequently allows sea water (and therefore nutrients) to move upwards, and fresh water to flush downwards during snow-melt. This produces favourable conditions for algal growth. The third method of ice formation occurs when free crystals form where conditions are sheltered and still. Phytoplankton is trapped among these crystals and incorporated into the ice layer.

Later in the summer, as the ice decays, it gradually becomes riddled with holes — like Gruyère cheese — which allows further nutrient exchange and the spread of algae.

Initially the sea ice contains about 30 per cent sea water, but by the end of winter this has fallen to 15 per cent. In early winter sea ice may be only 0.3 metres thick, but as much as two to three metres in late spring or early summer. Little, however, is known about maximum winter thicknesses and much research remains to be done.

The chemistry of sea ice also changes with the seasons. Melted ice cores which have been extracted vary from zero to 3 per cent salinity, while brine collected from holes drilled in sea ice can range from 6·4 to 12·4 per cent. Like the brine content, the nutrients taken from these cores fluctuate wildly. In summer, remarkably high levels of ammonia are found (far above those found in seawater), as well as high concentrations of nitrate and phosphate. This suggests the presence of a unique food chain of micro-organisms adapted to low temperatures and high salinity.

opposite
Pancake ice.

Frost flower on recently frozen sea ice showing its delicate crystal structure.

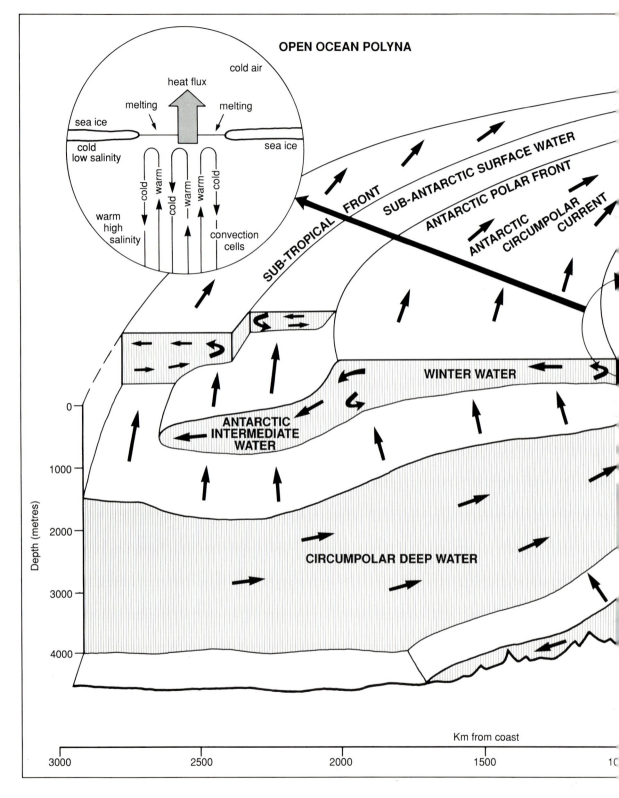

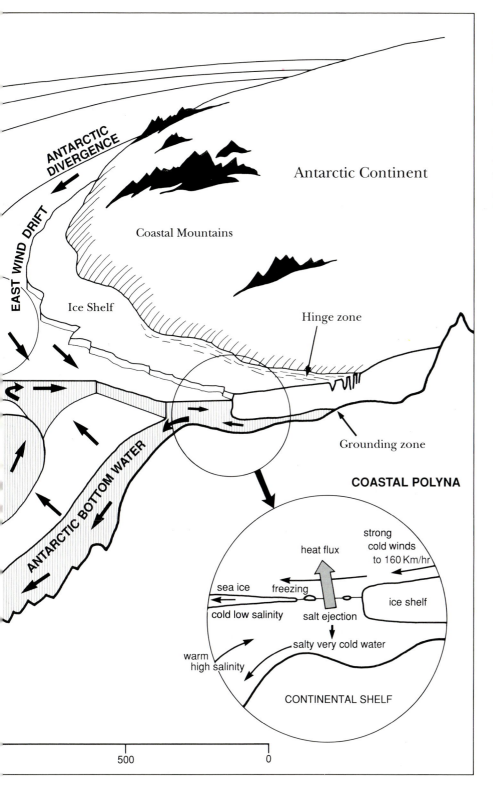

The currents and water masses of the Southern Ocean. Insets indicate processes: in a coastal polyna over the continental shelf, a sea ice factory; and in an open ocean polyna, where upwelling of warmer water promotes melting of the ice pack.

ANTARCTIC DIVERGENCE

EAST WIND DRIFT

Antarctic Continent

Coastal Mountains

Ice Shelf

Hinge zone

Grounding zone

ANTARCTIC BOTTOM WATER

COASTAL POLYNA

strong
cold winds
to 160 Km/hr

heat flux

sea ice   freezing

ice shelf

cold low salinity   salt ejection

salty very cold water

warm
high salinity

CONTINENTAL SHELF

500   0

Polynas

Consolidated pack ice in the Weddell Sea; the chaotic surface is complemented by an even more complex structure underneath which provides a habitat for marine life.

The most typical forms of sea ice are the floes, which range from a metre or so in diameter up to several miles across in consolidated pack ice. This pack ice does not have a continuous surface, but contains a random pattern of cracks (known as leads) and larger areas of open water. These open waters can be as much as 100 kilometres across. Where such large openings occur on a regular basis they are known as polynas. When polynas occur in cold water conditions over the continental shelf (especially where offshore winds are strong) they become a kind of ice factory, producing massive

amounts of new sea ice which is then blown offshore. This type of polyna can be found along most of the Antarctic coastline.

In a complementary way heat also escapes from the sea to the atmosphere through large holes in the blanket of sea ice. This heat has entered the oceans in temperate latitudes and been carried by ocean currents to the

The ice cliff of a fringing glacier at the entrance to Lemaire Channel, Antarctic Peninsula.

45

Tabular iceberg in the Weddell Sea surrounded by frost smoke caused by cold air coming into contact with relatively warm sea water.

Antarctic, where upwelling and low level winds bring it to the surface. One manifestation of the escaping heat is the 'frost smoke' visible to an observer, where warm deep water reaches the surface and is exposed to the very cold air. The role of open-ocean polynas in this cycle of heating and cooling is thought to be crucial to climatic changes on a truly global scale.

A second kind of polyna, is the open ocean polyna, created and maintained by local convective cells driven by upward-flowing, warm, deep water and sinking cold surface water; a very large one, the Weddell Polyna, formed in the winters of 1974, 1975 and 1976 but has not been seen since. Its maximum extent was 300,000 square kilometres.

LIFE OF THE LAND AND INLAND WATERS

Terrestrial vegetation

The fossil record of Antarctica shows that it had a much richer flora in the distant past, but as the climate deteriorated this lush vegetation disappeared. At first the ice expanded to cover a much greater area than it does today, but then it retreated again leaving small bare areas of land which were subsequently colonised by plants. But this recolonisation was hampered by the cold climate and the broad barrier of the Southern Ocean. This had the unusual effect of encouraging only those plants that reproduce by spores, and discouraged seed-producing plants.

Today Antarctica supports at least 340 different kinds of plant, a number which includes roughly 200 lichens, 85 mosses, 28 types of toadstool, 25 liverworts — and, in the maritime Antarctic, two kinds of flowering plants — plus an unknown number of algae. In the sub-Antarctic (for instance on the island of South Georgia) there is a wider, richer range of vegetation, which includes nearly thirty (mainly introduced) flowering plants.

Many of the lichens are native to the Antarctic, but most of the mosses (some of which can also be found in the Arctic) have arrived since the last Ice Age. Antarctica's restricted flora is hardly surprising, considering its exceptionally cold and arid climate, and it is instructive to consider the increasing variety of plant life towards the milder regions surrounding the continent.

Continental Antarctica

The high central plateau of Greater Antarctica is arguably the most inhospitable environment on Earth. With year-round temperatures well below 0°C there is virtually no free water, and since water is essential to life, much of the central ice cap is sterile. Nevertheless, bacteria, yeasts and some lichens have been found on bare, north-facing slopes of nunataks near

Toadstools growing amongst mosses and liverwort on Signy Island, South Orkney Islands.

Endolithic plants growing within sandstone rock in the dry valleys, Victoria Land. The black layer is a lichen, the white layer a fungus and the green layer an algal growth.

the South Pole, where there is some small degree of shelter. But these are uncommon, and much of Antarctica, even much further north, is devoid of life. In such situations it is all too easy for human activity to introduce unwanted microbes, even when precautions are taken.

Some of the Earth's most remarkable life-forms are found in the dry valleys and on Antarctica's high, hostile central plateau. These are the crypto-endolithic communities, which actually live inside solid rock. These communities are made up of lichens, fungi and algae which gradually evolved together as their shared environment deteriorated. The age of some of these communities can range from 750 to several thousand years.

Crypto-endolithic communities exist within minute cracks in the rock or even between the crystals of more porous marbles, sandstones, and granites.

They live on very small amounts of water, leached from melting snow. Algae, fungi and lichens live together, one type to each layer, blue-green algae living deepest and lichens within one millimetre of the surface.

The maritime Antarctic

Of all the maritime Antarctic regions, Signy Island in the South Orkneys has been studied by far the most intensely, over a period of 30 years. This island has a small permanent ice cap, coloured red, green or yellow in summer by patches of algae in the snow. Half of the ice-free surface of Signy Island is covered with lichens, and mosses are quite common, but Antarctica's two flowering plants are less abundant.

Snow slopes
coloured pink by
the proliferation of
snow algae during
the spring melt.

Freshwater lakes at
Signy Island; the
nearer lake is
Heywood Lake
which is enriched
by excreta from
seals and seabirds.

52

The low-growing lichens on the sea coasts, some of which can live four thousand years or more here often grow in colourful stripes, from black and brown around the bases of the cliffs to bright yellow and orange at their tops. Among the mosses here, the tall moss turf is one of the most striking forms of Antarctic vegetation. This forms peat banks up to three metres deep, whose bases regularly date back more than five thousand years. Even apparently dead black moss peat which has been buried by ice for a century will regenerate when it becomes exposed.

Because all these plant forms grow very slowly in Antarctica's cold conditions, they are very vulnerable to disturbance, particularly trampling: on Signy Island there are human footprints clearly visible decades after they were made.

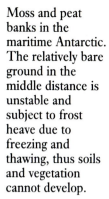

Moss and peat banks in the maritime Antarctic. The relatively bare ground in the middle distance is unstable and subject to frost heave due to freezing and thawing, thus soils and vegetation cannot develop.

The sub-Antarctic

Although the climate of the sub-Antarctic islands is still quite severe compared to most parts of the world, the influence of the Southern Ocean means that it is mild in comparison to that of continental Antarctica. Environmental conditions throughout this ring of remote islands are also determined by the date since they were last covered by permanent ice. The evidence suggests that the last major glacial retreat began between 11 and 12 thousand years ago in South Georgia, which means its soils and those on other islands are relatively young.

The flora of these islands is richer and more conspicuous than in the

regions to the south, and includes large flowering plants. The flowering plants most resemble those found to their west: South Georgia's, for instance, resemble those in Tierra del Fuego, and Macquarie Island's those in Australasia. Birds are probably the main agents of dispersal, and many sub-Antarctic plants show adaptations to promote their carriage in this way. For instance some fruits are hooked, while others are edible, and some seeds have sticky coatings.

Pollen is also widely blown by westerly winds, but the only plants spread by wind this way are probably the ferns, whose spores are very light. Many other plants have been introduced by man, like the dandelions and chickweed in South Georgia which grow around abandoned whaling stations.

Lichens are a major component of Antarctic vegetation. These colourful species on coastal rocks benefit from nutrients introduced by seaspray and nearby seabird colonies.

The delicate fronds of the fern, *Blechnum penna-marina*; it is the dominant species in the fernbrake vegetation type of the sub-Antarctic.

One of the most successful introductions is the grass *Poa annua*. Tussock grass another *Poa* species, which relies on sea-spray to survive, helps South Georgia's reindeer to over-winter, and provides a habitat for burrowing petrels, rats and mice. On seepage slopes with shallow peat, and deep-peat bogs, rushes and mosses grow, while pools may have floating swamp vegetation at their edge.

There are no annual species in the sub-Antarctic, and even the normally annual grass *Poa annua* adopts a perennial life cycle here. Other typical adaptations are vegetative reproduction, food storage organs and flowers that are formed a season before they are needed.

Land animals

With a few conspicuous exceptions, Antarctica's land animals are confined to microbes and to a few small invertebrates. Because of their tiny size, and because almost all of them exist in plant litter, moss banks, peat, soil, and in the micro-climates under stones, they are much harder to study than the plants. The only feasible method is to take samples of soil or litter and extract the animals in the laboratory.

Only a few of the warmer islands of the sub-Antarctic support earthworms, land snails, insects and spiders. Antarctica's impoverished flora and fauna means that their interactions are much simpler than elsewhere and, what is more, are virtually undisturbed by man or the effects of pollution. Nevertheless a total of 387 invertebrates have so far been discovered in the sub-Antarctic, 127 in the maritime Antarctic and 107 on the continent itself (many of which occur in more than one of these zones).

Postage stamps of the Falkland Islands Dependencies, showing animals of the maritime Antarctic. Clockwise from top left: springtail, *Cryptopygus*; mite, *Alaskozetes*; predatory mite, *Gamasellus*; spider, *Notiomaso*; beetle, *Hydromedion*; and midge *Parochlus*.

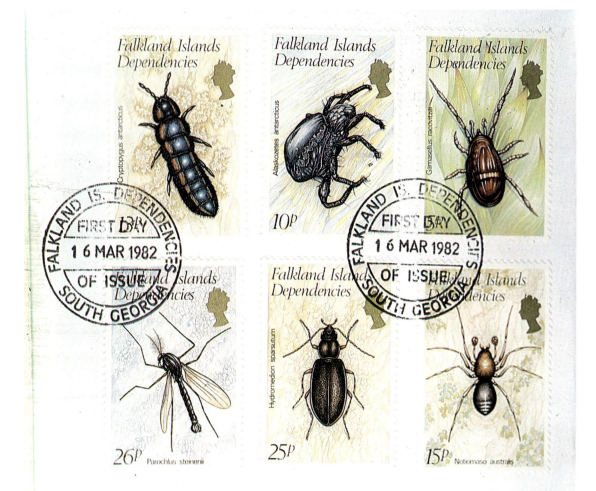

Simplest are the protozoans, single-celled micro-organisms which come in a variety of forms. Their number decreases with increasing latitude, but densities of 35,000 testate (enclosed within a shell or test) protozoans have been found in one square centimetre of soil.

Next in complexity come the rotifers, less than half a millimetre long, which need at least a film of water in which to live, but can survive some drying out. Only 15 of the world's 700 known rotifers exist in the Antarctic, but they can live in concentrations of up to 931,000 per square metre. Similar to the rotifers are the tardigrades, which have adapted well to low temperatures and severe desiccation, and sometimes achieve densities of 14 million individuals per square metre.

More successful still is a group of small worms called nematodes, one type of which is predatory; but even nematodes get eaten in their turn by a kind of fungus and a fast-moving mite. Small white worms and land snails are found on both the sub-Antarctic islands and (in less profusion) in the maritime Antarctic. At Macquarie Island, European slugs have been introduced by man and apparently thrive in this relatively mild climate.

Compared to other regions of the world, insects are scarce in Antarctica. Of 67 species recorded in continental Antarctica and the maritime Antarctic, most are parasites dependent on a host and only 22 roam free. Wingless springtails are also found along with flies and midges.

Other insects include the parasitic sucking lice which live on seals, fleas which live in birds' nests and biting lice which gather at the warm bases of birds' feathers. Most of the Antarctic beetles are introductions, over half being herbivorous weevils. All 14 types of spider known are restricted to the sub-Antarctic, but of this number, four, which live in South Georgia, are the most southerly in the world.

Antarctic mites are a large and relatively well-known group, mostly endemic to the region. Some 70 species are known, with a similar number from South Georgia. They include the feather mites on birds and a specialised group which live in the nasal passages of seals. Among the mites is the most southerly-living animal on Earth, *Nanorchestes antarcticus*, found even on those nunataks (rocky outcrops) nearest to the Pole.

Food webs

Since the Antarctic species are so few, food chains or webs are fairly simple. The primary consumers are the protozoans, rotifers, tardigrades, nematodes, mites and collembola, which feed on bacteria, algae and fungi. There are a few predators, the fast-moving yellow mite, *Gamasellus racovitzi* being one.

In the sub-Antarctic food webs are more complex, the primary consumers being joined by beetles and fly larvae. Here the predators include spiders, carnivorous beetles and mites.

All life in the Southern Ocean is linked within a great food web, based on phytoplankton and microplankton. Zoo-plankton, squid and fish are the food base for the more conspicuous birds, seals and whales. Migration and mortality due to commercial hunting removes material from the system. The foodwebs of land and freshwater are very simple in comparison and lack higher vertebrates (grazing mammals and fish).

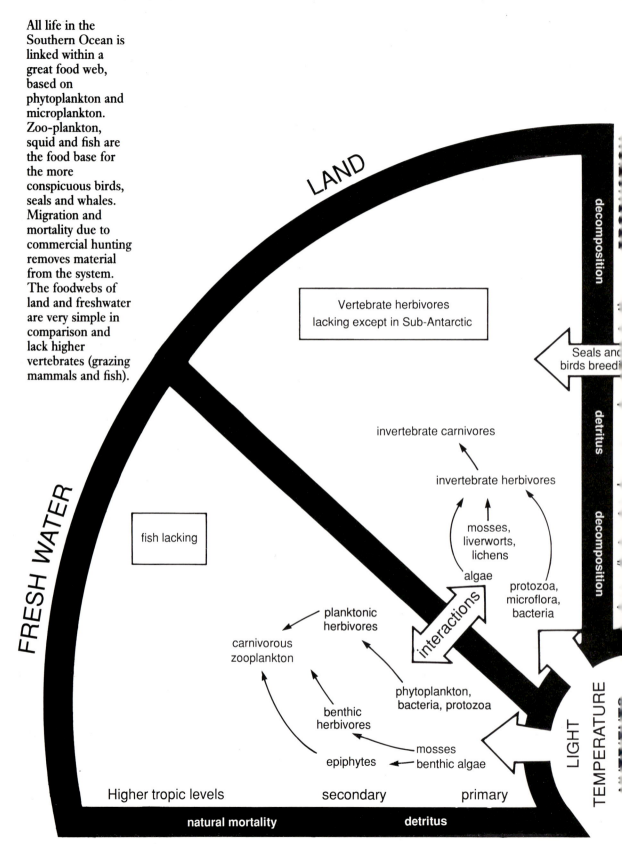

LAND

FRESH WATER

decomposition

Vertebrate herbivores
lacking except in Sub-Antarctic

Seals and
birds breedi

detritus

decomposition

invertebrate carnivores

invertebrate herbivores

fish lacking

mosses,
liverworts,
lichens

algae

protozoa,
microflora,
bacteria

planktonic
herbivores

carnivorous
zooplankton

interactions

phytoplankton,
bacteria, protozoa

benthic
herbivores

mosses

epiphytes ← benthic algae

LIGHT

TEMPERATURE

Higher tropic levels   secondary   primary

natural mortality   detritus

Seals and birds
breed on land and
together with
seaspray contribute
to a marine
influence on land
and freshwater
systems.

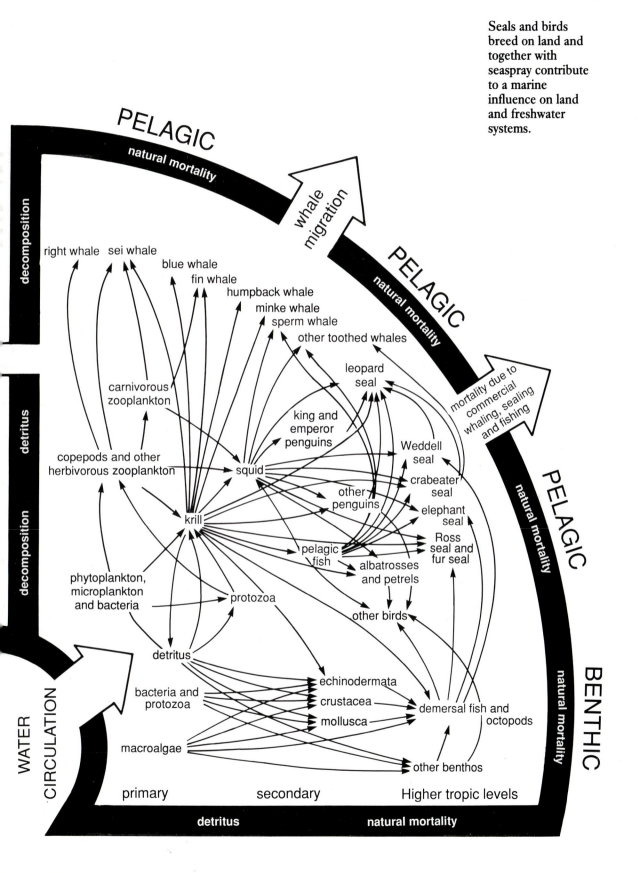

Adaptations

All life ultimately depends on the presence of free water, which makes the sub-zero temperatures of the Antarctic's land extremely difficult for living things, since almost all its water is frozen into ice. Within the sea, free water is obviously no problem as long as temperatures remain above -1.9°C: below this even sea-water freezes. The small temperature variations of freshwaters (from 0°C to 6°C) also favour life. On land, however, living organisms are exposed to a temperature range as great as -59°C to +25°C. Of course, in inland waters, just as in the sea, life is hardly limited by a lack of free water, and in high southern latitudes fresh water often supports much more life than the surrounding land, although some very salty lakes may have temperatures as low as -55°C, supporting little or no life.

The yellow predatory mite *Gamasellus racovitzai* attacking an Antarctic springtail, *Cryptopygus antarcticus* about one millimetre long – its main source of food.

Under such conditions it is not surprising that many land creatures have developed strategies to cope with the potentially lethal low temperatures. One group of animals avoid freezing by supercooling themselves down as far as -40°C to -50°C, but this is the lower limit for survival.

In all animals the contents of the gut (food particles, grit, sand or dust) provide the focus for freezing, so collembolans and mites, to take just two examples, feed when the temperature rises and they fast when it begins to fall. A second small group of organisms have improved on this ability by producing anti-freeze substances which protect their tissues and cells. In the mite *Alaskozetes* glycerol begins to gather in the tissues below 0°C, and as

The mite *Alaskozetes antarcticus* lives under rocks and lichens, and among algae; it makes antifreezes to aid overwintering.

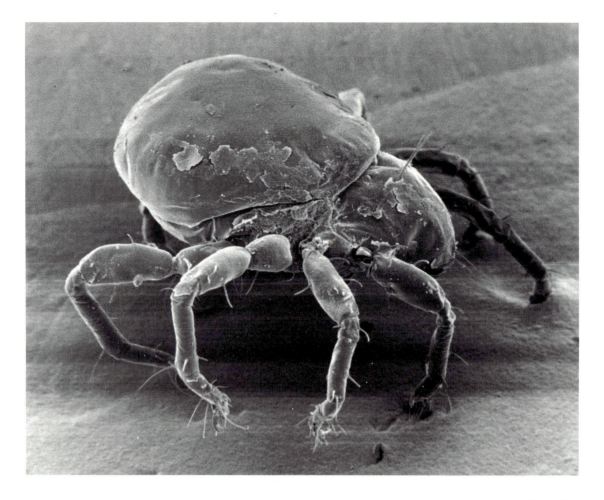

A herbivorous mite, *Alaskozetes antarcticus*. Slow-moving, armoured and just over one millimetre long it is one of the largest Antarctic terrestrial invertebrates.

its concentration increases, so the mite's freezing point lowers (just like adding anti-freeze to a water-cooled car engine). Anti-freezes are also found in the collembolan *Cryptopygus* and the flightless midge, *Belgica antarctica*.

Another strategy is to increase the metabolic rate following exposure to cold, which counteracts the slowing effects of lower temperatures. Animals are also able to postpone their development if environmental conditions are unfavourable. As a result their life span may be extended: for example the collembolans — which in warmer climates produce one or more generations every year — can live to three years old. The midges too have flexible life cycles, so larvae can be found at any time of year, and their life span, too, can extend to two or three years.

One final method of adaptation is the capacity to survive without oxygen for long periods. At some times of the year, Antarctica's tiny land organisms may become entirely surrounded by a layer of ice. Under such conditions their oxygen supply will soon run out, but experiments have shown that some species can exist for several days, or even months without it.

Life in inland waters

Although Antarctica contains nine tenths of the world's fresh water, very little of it is in liquid form and there are few ice-free areas where lakes can develop; nor are there any true streams or rivers. Antarctic lakes are frozen for much of the year, turning them effectively into closed systems, which means, however, that they are less affected by seasonal climatic change than lakes in lower latitudes.

There are many different types of inland waters in Antarctica, which range from small fresh-water pools to large and very salty lakes. The most intensively studied inland waters in the Antarctic are sixteen lakes on Signy Island. Since their formation the food webs of these lakes have increased in complexity. So far scientists have recorded 24 species of phytoplankton, 96 species of algae, 82 protozoans and 39 rotifers. Much of the life found in any of these waters is common to the land around them, for many algae and invertebrates are equally at home in pools or lakes, or the free-water layers of moss cushions and other vegetation.

At least 17 large lakes have been revealed beneath three to four thousand metres of ice, which could be anything up to five million years old. The physical, chemical — and possibly living — components of these lakes are unknown: one can only speculate that primitive life may exist within them, since research on the Antarctic ice sheet has demonstrated that microbes have successfully survived for millenia within the ice.

Bottom-growing aquatic mosses and green algae are an important feature of nutrient-poor lakes on Signy Island, South Orkney Islands.

Sub-Antarctic lakes

Most of the sub-Antarctic islands are extremely remote and so their lakes are isolated from other fresh-water communities by long stretches of ocean. The exception is South Georgia, which belongs to a chain of islands stretching from Tierra del Fuego along the Scotia arc to the Antarctic Peninsula. The sub-Antarctic climate is generally mild and it is unusual for lakes to be ice-covered for long. Relatively high air temperatures also mean that summer water temperatures (particularly in shallow pools) are correspondingly high (up to 14°C). Rainfall can also be as high as 2.5 metres a year (on Marion Island): in South Georgia it has also shown a remarkable increase of 33 per cent from 1905 to 1976.

Little sustained research has been done on the sub-Antarctic lakes. They are often much more complex than those further south, and their surrounding catchment areas are better vegetated. Their own aquatic vegetation can also be relatively rich, and they can be fringed with rooted and floating plants around their shores.

The freshwater fairy shrimp, *Branchinecta gainii* overwinters in the egg stage.

Saline lakes

As evaporation or isolation slowly increases the salinity of a lake, its environment becomes more and more hostile to both fresh-water and marine life. One extreme example is Don Juan Pond in Victoria Land, which contains enough salt to reduce its theoretical freezing point to -48°C, 25 times the freezing point of sea-water.

Lake Vanda, also in the dry valleys of Victoria Land, is a stratified lake, fed primarily by melt-water from glaciers. Its freshwater surface is separated from a virtually sterile lower salty level, but because of its low temperature and persistent ice cover even the fresh water supports little life.

Another interesting stratified system exists in Ablation Lake, on Alexander Island, locked behind the dam of the George VI Ice Shelf. Ablation Lake is 100 kilometres from open water, but its tidal rhythm reveals that its lower saline layer is connected directly to the open sea. Fresh-water crustaceans live in its surface layer: at the same time, in the salt water below, marine copepods and the fish *Trematomus bernacchii* have been found.

Shore and Sea Floor Life

Bergy-bits and brash ice scour the Antarctic shores.

The Antarctic we have seen so far appears to be a hostile land of ice and snow, of sub-zero temperatures, high winds and blizzards, a land of white or grey horizons surrounded by a leaden sea. Yet underneath the surface of that dark ocean is another world, in places as rich and strange and colourful as any tropical reef. Here low stable temperatures support a rich diversity of life, including animals which far outgrow their warm-water counterparts.

Yet for all the richness in the sea, the polar shores are very inhospitable, scoured as they are by fast ice, pack ice, brash ice and bergy bits from glaciers and icebergs. Large icebergs, eighty per cent submerged, can carve scars on ocean floors 150 metres down or more. More than 45 per cent of the Antarctic coastline is fringed with glaciers or ice shelves, but even where the shores are bare the ice abrasion means that no perennial seaweeds grow, except in narrow cracks between the rocks. At lower latitudes in the sub-Antarctic less ice abrades the shore, and in South Georgia dense beds of giant kelp grow to lengths of over 15 metres.

The limpets, mussels and barnacles common to temperate coasts are largely absent, though Antarctic limpets, which graze on algae and migrate to deeper water in winter, can survive short periods at −20°C.

Immediately below the tidal coast are the shallow rocky waters known as the sub-littoral zone. Iceberg scouring also affects this zone, but where this is less prevalent worms, prawns, sea slugs, sea spiders, sea urchins, starfish, sea cucumbers, sea squirts, pale yellow coral and red and purple sea anemones populate the rocks and mud. There are also at least 300 varieties of Antarctic sponges, including one a metre tall, which grows only in far deeper waters elsewhere in the world.

A sea anemone and sponge in a sheltered part of the sublittoral at Signy Island, South Orkney Islands.

Deep water flora and fauna

Below depths of 30 metres the temperatures of the Antarctic seas have little more effect on flora and fauna than those of deep waters in any other ocean in the world. The sea floors, though, are covered not by river-borne sediment, but by an annual 500 million tonnes of rock and debris excavated by glaciers on the land, and deposited by icebergs. Beyond the limits of the pack ice and the continental slopes are the abyssal plains and one extremely deep ocean rift, the South Sandwich Trench, which reaches a depth of 8,620 metres, almost the same vertical height as Mount Everest.

The lack of light in deep water means there are no living plants, since light is essential for photosynthesis. But where the sea bed is rocky there are far higher numbers of animals than are commonly found in other oceans, probably because the rocky bottom provides a good anchorage for corals and sponges. Among the mobile animals are molluscs, feather stars, unique ten and twelve-legged sea spiders, starfish (including the many-armed sunburst starfish) and above all the highly mobile brittle stars, or ophiuroids. These are known to gather in vast local concentrations (up to 100 million per square kilometre) in the Ross Sea. Sponges and some corals remain abundant at depths of up to one kilometre.

Colourful starfish are abundant in Antarctic waters.

Life on a sheltered rock face, 10 metres deep off Signy Island. The surface is covered with yellow encrusting sponges and the pink alga *Lithothamnion*, with anemones, limpets, starfish and sea urchins. Long stalks of the yellow *Primnoella* hang down.

Life beneath the ice shelves

Circumstantial evidence suggests that even beneath the thick ice shelves remote from the open sea there may be relatively rich animal communities. White Island, in the middle of the 70 metre thick Ross Ice Shelf, and 22 kilometres from the nearest open water has long been known for its thriving population of well-fed Weddell seals. A solitary seal — possibly the same individual — has been seen from time to time at Ablation Lake, a hundred kilometres from the open sea and separated from it by an ice shelf 100 metres thick.

More mysteriously still, the bodies of a gigantic fish (*Dissostichus maw-*

soni), sea urchins and other seabed animals have been found on the surface of the Ross Ice Shelf, far distant from the open sea. The most likely explanation is that these animals were frozen to the ice's underside, and were then gradually transported to the surface as ice formed below and was lost above.

In 1977 a hole was drilled through the Ross Ice Shelf, 450 kilometres from open water, and television cameras revealed a scattering of seafloor swimming animals such as copepods and euphausiids, mysids, amphipods, isopods and two fish. It is thought that life can only be sustained so far beneath the shelf by currents bringing detritus in from its edge.

Growth, size and reproduction

As the ancient supercontinent, Gondwana, broke up, isolating Antarctica from the warmer oceans of the world, its progressive cooling critically affected the physiology of invertebrate animals. Since this was such a gradual process, with temperatures falling only 0.003°C every thousand years, these invertebrates had ample time to adapt. Cold water slows their growth and reproductive rates, but it also reduces the amount of energy required to live, so it has its economic advantages. And since the amount of energy needed for invertebrates and fish to grow, breed and move is similar from the tropics to the poles, cold conditions promote greater metabolic efficiencies. It's rather anthropocentric, after all, to assume that warm environments are less stressful than cold ones: it can be argued, on the contrary, that (for marine invertebrates at least), tropical environments cause more stress, since so much energy is wasted on body maintenance.

A colourful sea slug on a muddy bottom off Signy Island.

Rates of calcification (the formation of bones or shells) are also reduced by cold, so Antarctica is poor in the types of marine organism which need large amounts of calcium for their growth. In this context it is interesting to speculate whether oceanic squids, with their much reduced shells (compared to their ammonite ancestors) evolved in these cold waters.

Growth in most polar marine animals is slow, if averaged through the year, but it can be very rapid in short bursts when food supplies are plentiful. Since slowly-growing invertebrates reach greater sizes than faster-growing ones, the waters of Antarctica have the largest proportion of giants and the smallest number of dwarfs of any oceanic region. One advantage of larger

The giant isopod *Glyptonotus*, an ubiquitous omnivore and scavenger.

size is that more surviving offspring are produced, though the process takes longer. Slow growth is also associated with longevity, and a limpet named *Nacella* may live 100 years, whilst sponges can live for several centuries.

All this evidence suggests that summer food availability, and not low temperature, is the crucial factor in the growth of marine animals in the Antarctic. In general the life cycle is timed to fit this seasonal cycle, so eggs are laid in winter and hatching occurs in spring to coincide with the phytoplankton bloom. Up to three summer feeding periods may be necessary to produce viable eggs or sperm, so individuals may have three

The giant ten-legged sea spider, *Decalopodium antarcticum*.

generations of eggs inside their bodies, to be spawned in three successive seasons. In Antarctic species brood size is smaller, eggs are larger, and larvae more advanced on hatching than in comparable species from warmer waters, giving them a better chance of survival.

The seabed of the Antarctic supports a great diversity of life (or benthos), much more so than the younger Arctic. Across a range of eight animal groups, 3,133 marine Antarctic species have been recorded compared to only 1,311 in the Arctic, and this despite the fact that the benthos of the Antarctic is far less known than that of the Arctic.

Evolution on the ocean floor

Before the present glaciation there were extensive shallow seas between Lesser and Greater Antarctica, and fossils from the late Cretaceous and Eocene periods imply a rich shallow-water fauna in this part of Gondwana. This ranged from corals to fish, including almost all the groups which still exist. It is now believed these long-extant shallows enabled many new species to evolve, which later moved to warmer or deeper waters to continue their development. Most of these former shallow seas are now covered by the grounded ice cap, which eradicated any life, or by ice shelves with little life beneath them. Whether former glaciations scraped the continental shelf free of life is not known, nor whether in some deeper areas seabed animals survived and underwent adaptive evolutions.

The delicate tracery of a sea cucumber's gills.

Today, in contrast to the ancient gentle temperature gradient between high and low latitudes, there are great differences between the temperatures at the poles and at the tropics. Seasonal surface changes in the warmer oceans may be as high as 20°C, but in polar waters this range is much reduced, from roughly -1.9°C to 4.0°C at most. Polar organisms show fine-tuning to this stability, but they have little tolerance to sudden change. Cold waters contain more oxygen than warm, though ice-shelves may diminish it. Salinity is reduced near melting icebergs or in surface waters during spring and summer. All this results in species densities at 5-75 metres of four times those off North America, while Antarctica's long isolation has produced a high proportion of endemic types. In some groups this reaches 95 per cent, but in the Antarctic region as a whole the figure is 72 per cent.

Mating activities of the Antarctic limpet, *Nacella concinna* include this unusual 'stacking' behaviour.

81

THE OCEANIC PLANKTON

Diver with large
comb jelly
(Ctenophore).

Phyto- and microplankton

The unique properties of the Southern Ocean have noticeable effects on the biology and distribution of planktonic life. The most important factors are the waxing and waning of the pack ice zone, the lack of light for half the year, the extensive cloud cover and the role of the various water masses.

The phytoplankton (plankton consisting of plants) is dominated by diatoms, dinoflagellates and silicoflagellates. Diatoms are enclosed in robust siliceous containers, either drum-shaped (centric) or boat-shaped (pennate), and often intricately sculpted. Nearly one hundred species have been recorded in Antarctica. The dinoflagellates are much smaller, mostly lacking in external coverings, and so more vulnerable to damage; silicoflagellates, however, have internal skeletons, which like the shells of diatoms reveal great beauty under the microscope.

Plankton abundance is greatest during summer, and where diatom blooms occur they can be quite conspicuous, like a thick pea soup which spreads for miles across the open ocean. One such bloom contained 1.4 million cells per litre at depths of five metres. But different communities reach peaks at different times, and all are prone to the prodigious movements of Antarctic seas, with their upwellings, great waves and gale-force winds which churn up the sea to a depth of 60-80 metres.

In recent years the importance of microplankton has been reevaluated. Not only are they thought to represent three quarters of the oceanic chlorophyll, but in Antarctica itself they make a major contribution to the food chain, since like diatoms they feed the whale-supporting krill.

The drifting sea ice zone

It is only in the last few years that powerful ice-breakers have allowed the exploration of the waters underneath the drifting ice, with the aid of scuba-diving and small, remote-controlled submersibles. The results of these studies are extremely exciting, for they open up a whole new environment, and one on a vast scale. At its maximum seasonal extent, the pack ice covers

Ice floes overturned by the passage of a ship reveal the brown layer of ice-associated algae.

an area seven times that of all the tropical rainforests in the world, and twice that of the tropical and temperate forests combined. The expansion and contraction of this pack ice is the largest seasonal process in the oceans of the world, creating an additional habitat for life of 16 million square kilometres every winter, which disappears each summer.

At first, pack ice's undersurface may be fairly smooth, but cracking and refreezing eventually results in a very complex layered mass, as full of holes and crevices as Swiss cheese. This kind of floating environment is rare in the open ocean, and perhaps can only be compared with the Sargasso Sea, where floating weeds provide a home for ocean life. Algae attach themselves to the underside of the ice, while the caverns protect small algae-grazing animals like krill from the predators of the open sea.

When pack ice forms it contains, like the winter ocean, little suspended matter or life, but soon it is colonised by algae and bacteria, and as the ice breaks up and forms again they get amalgamated. These algae and bacteria have adapted to light's low penetration of the ice, and can exist on less than one per cent of the light which falls upon the surface. They are also adapted to cold and super-salty conditions, for winter temperatures may fall to -10°C and salinities rise to 150 per thousand (seawater is normally 34 per thousand).

Amphipod crustaceans cluster on the under-surface of fast ice.

Zooplankton

Zooplankton is the animal plankton which feeds on the minute plants of the phytoplankton. It includes small crustaceans, the Antarctic krill, arrow worms, pelagic gastropods (like slugs and snails), jellyfish and fish larvae. Strictly speaking plankton drifts passively in the water, but some species referred to as zooplankton are actually quite mobile, and should be more properly defined as nekton (free-swimming organisms). Studies have concentrated on the krill, *Euphausia superba* because of its enormous ecological interest and importance, but there are ten other types of krill. (Their general name derives from the Norwegian name for whale food.)

Of the other plankton animals, *Salpa thompsoni* is particularly fascinating, as its reproduction can be both sexual and asexual, producing two quite different forms, one solitary and one aggregate. The solitary offspring grows from embryos released in March and April, and they form the winter population's nucleus. But then in spring each individual animal produces chains of up to 800 buds, setting off a population explosion. Finally, at the end of each summer each individual within the aggregate conceives a single egg, which is released when 4-5 millimetres long. This unusual process brings about an 'alternation of generations' within this species.

Cell of the characteristic Antarctic diatom, *Thalassiosira antarctica*; the tubes produce threads which join cells together. Diameter about 40 microns.

Internal view of half of the silica skeleton of the endemic Antarctic diatom, *Nitzschia kerguelensis*, about 50 microns long.

Vertical migrations

Zooplankton species tend to move in vertical directions between the north and southward flowing water masses, either daily, seasonally or as part of their life cycle. Some types spend the summer in the northward flowing Antarctic Surface Water, then descend into the Circumpolar or Warm Deep Water for the winter months. Others spend the day in the Circumpolar Deep Water and the night nearer the surface.

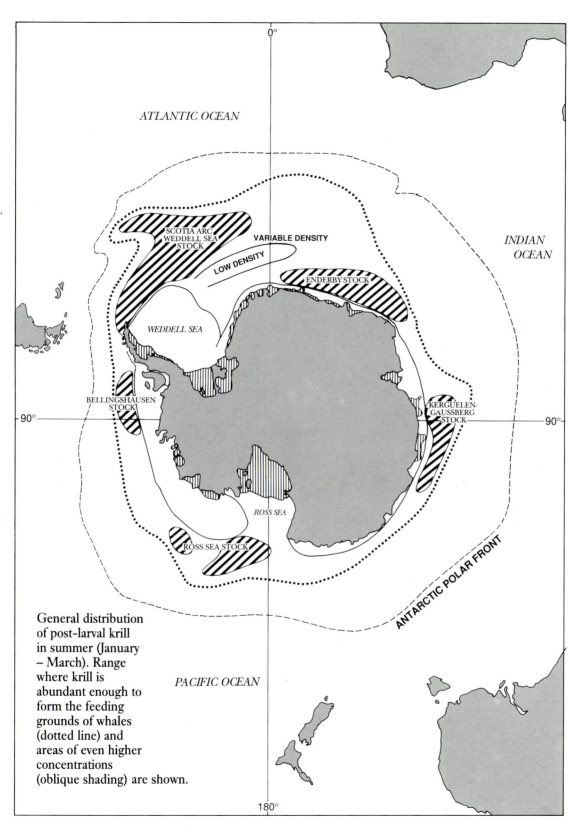

0°

ATLANTIC OCEAN

INDIAN OCEAN

SCOTIA ARC
WEDDELL SEA
STOCK

VARIABLE DENSITY

LOW DENSITY

ENDERBY STOCK

WEDDELL SEA

BELLINGSHAUSEN
STOCK

90°

KERGUELEN-
GAUSSBERG
STOCK

90°

ROSS SEA

ROSS SEA STOCK

ANTARCTIC POLAR FRONT

General distribution
of post-larval krill
in summer (January
– March). Range
where krill is
abundant enough to
form the feeding
grounds of whales
(dotted line) and
areas of even higher
concentrations
(oblique shading) are shown.

PACIFIC OCEAN

180°

Fine structure of
the krill feeding
basket showing in
order of size setae,
setules and
microsetules.
Spaces between
setules about 10-15
microns.

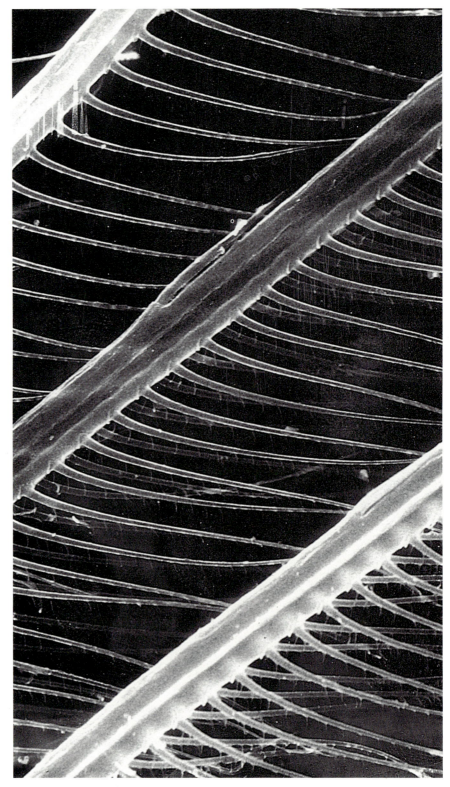

The Antarctic krill

Some 600,000 billion (million million) individual Antarctic krill spread out across five per cent of the world's oceans in densities of roughly 19 million to a square kilometre. The total weight of krill on Earth is thought to exceed that of the entire human race: something like 650 million tonnes.

The krill is a shrimp-like crustacean about 6-7 centimetres long, which swims forwards with five pairs of paddle-like legs, or for short periods quickly backwards using its tail. They have a complicated feeding apparatus resembling a tiny fishing net, which filters and extracts a wide range of organisms from the water, but they have to work hard to gather adequate amounts of phytoplankton food in the waters of Antarctica.

Strangely, krill are badly suited to their habitat, for unlike other zooplankton they are heavier than water, and have to struggle constantly to remain afloat. They hover in the water at an angle of 55 degrees, continuously paddling, (rather like small helicopters), or jump jets and move forward by altering this angle.

Very few weak krill survive, for if they falter, or oxygen levels decrease slightly in the water, or they fail to find enough food, they plunge rapidly under their own weight to depths where they are unable to stay alive. Most krill suffocate at depths of 250 metres and more because they need a lot of oxygen, which is depleted at these depths.

But this is not the only oddity of krill physiology. Their metabolism, for example, works in reverse compared to most animals. The metabolic rate of most animals slows down as they increase in weight, but krill metabolism actually speeds up. This doesn't seem so odd when one knows that 40 per cent of their energy is expended simply on staying still.

Krill and the pack ice zone

During the winter most krill communities are over-roofed by pack ice, protecting them to some degree from predators. But this also means their winter habitat, amongst the caves and crevices that riddle the pack-ice covering, is radically different to their summer one. In winter krill can graze on algae growing on the undersurface of the ice, using their filter basket like a lawn-rake to scrape them off. They can also probably save energy by 'walking' on the ice rather than having to hover as they do in open water. Other strategies for overwintering may include a switch of diet, reduced metabolic demands and a reliance on reserves, but much further research has yet to be done.

Though krill are found all round Antarctica, several areas show particularly high concentrations, corresponding generally to eddies or gyres in the oceanic circulation. Whether or not these concentrations indicate separate reserves is an issue of critical importance to the way krill stocks are going to be maintained in the future. The largest concentration is found in the

Swimming
Antarctic Krill,
showing feeding
basket, stomachs
filled with green
diatoms and pink
pigmentation.

Weddell Gyre, and before so many whales were killed many congregated there, to feed in summer; seals and breeding colonies of birds are also more abundant in this region than elsewhere.

Krill spawning and growth

Krill spawn mainly during the summer months, and mature females spawn twice a year, laying between two and three thousand eggs on each occasion, which hatch at depths of 750 metres. As the larvae develop they slowly rise towards the surface, growing to six centimetres in two to three years.

Early studies set krill lifespans at two years, but now they are known to live

Comb jelly or
ctenophore.

much longer: krill confined to laboratories have lived for seven years. This
long lifespan is unusual, if not unique among planktonic life.

Despite its physiological disadvantages, adult krill are remarkably successful at taking advantage of the seasonal fluctuations of Southern Ocean
food. Part of their success depends on the lack of competition with fish like
herring, mackerel and capelin, which gives krill access to the largest feeding
area of any ocean in the world. Huge so-called super-swarms, containing up
to 2.1 million tonnes of krill across an area of 450 square kilometres, have
been detected by echo-sounding, though swarms comprising tens to
hundreds of tonnes are more usual. Fishing for krill is now big business and
trawlers can catch eight to twelve tonnes of krill an hour.

Other Planktonic animals

Compared to Antarctic krill, relatively little is known about the biology and ecology of other zooplankton species, but it is worth quickly summarising what information there is. Like the krill, most species grow fastest during summer, and to survive through the winter adopt a range of different strategies such as storing fat reserves within their bodies or overwintering in larval states. Omnivores have a relatively easier time finding enough food, and carnivores can take advantage of the fact that zooplankton numbers remain roughly level throughout the year.

The other zooplankton also display varied reproductive cycles, many developing through several seasons, or through different depths or temperatures of water. *Salpa thompsoni* has a curious alternation of generations already described.

Small medusa
(jellyfish).

OCEANIC SQUIDS AND FISH

Squids: origins and adaptations

Squids, cuttlefish and octopuses all belong to the Cephalopoda group of animals, and are allied to other molluscs like snails and slugs. These marine molluscs have evolved in great variety of form function and are widespread and numerous in the oceans of the world.

The squids began to evolve their advanced features before fishes, around 500 million years ago. Some of them are very streamlined, big-eyed, big brained and jet propelled. Like the more familiar octopuses they have tentacles with suckers and hooks.

The ancestors of present-day squids developed from ammonites and belemnites and other prehistoric molluscs, which had hard shells divided into gas-filled compartments to provide buoyancy. Over time, the shell flattened and muscle developed around it, allowing them to jet propel in short bursts, as well as giving them great manoeuvrability. They also developed fins and buoyancy mechanisms enabling them to live even in the greatest depths of water.

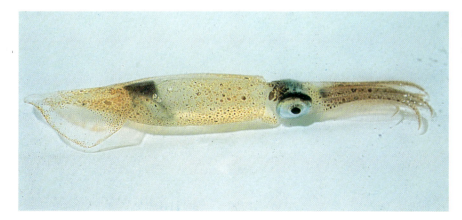

Todarodes is a common small Antarctic squid.

Brachioteuthis is another common Antarctic squid.

Jet propulsion requires a great deal of energy, so the food needs of squids are large. An alternative way of getting around the problem, however, uses far less energy: this involves producing a low-density liver-oil which makes them 'neutrally buoyant', liable neither to sink nor to float upwards — in other words, allowing them to hover in mid-water.

Another, even odder solution is to convert their waste gases into ammonia and to grow a jelly-like body. This limits the amount of oxygen they need and their jelly-like body can form a variety of shapes to reduce sinking rates: some types (included in the Cranchiidae) are almost spherical.

All cephalopods can change colour rapidly, thanks to a combination of highly reflective structures and colour-cells which can quickly expand or contract. This ability, like transparency in others, provides defensive camouflage for them in a wide variety of situations. Deep sea creatures tend to be black or red, because the water column absorbs most of the red light in the spectrum.

But squids also generate light to help them hide from predators. Since most light in the ocean comes from above, most objects cast some sort of shadow, which can be seen by predators. To compensate for this, light cells on the underside of some cephalopods give out light which matches that which could be expected to come from above at any given depth.

Light can be generated either biochemically or by encouraging light-emitting bacteria. Once produced, the light can be reflected, re-directed and concentrated by reflectors and lenses, and changed in wavelength by filters.

Another better known squid defence mechanism is black ink. This mixture of pigment (melanin), mucus — and sometimes also a chemical irritant — can act as a decoy shape (and sometimes blind a predator), while the squid escapes.

Squid lives

Very little is known of the biology and ecology of squids in general, and even less about their Antarctic representatives. To some extent, therefore, we have to assume certain similarities among all species, and this qualification must be borne in mind in what follows.

In the life history of squids, the usual spawning season lasts for more than six months, and the female, once mature, may spawn only once (or several times in one season) and then die. The eggs may be laid at depth in mid-water, on continental shelves or around islands and float towards the surface as they develop. Once hatched, the infant squids may migrate towards the surface at once, or wait until they are adults and ready to spawn.

Squids can grow as fast as the fastest growing fish, but their growth is dependent on water temperatures and their species type. Although the evidence is slight it is thought that most species live for only one or two years. Males mature quicker, and grow larger than females: certain males have been known to attain lengths of 20 metres.

Squids feed voraciously, using their tentacles, suckers and needle-sharp hooks to grasp their prey. Inside their mouths are two brown horny beaks, attached to powerful muscles, which can inflict fatal deep bites even on large fish. Many squids are cannibals, and in one species other squids are estimated to provide 35 per cent of their young's total diet.

Squids are extremely difficult to catch, because of their speed and vision, but they are known to be an important group in oceanic food webs, since they are found so frequently in the guts of fish, birds, seals and whales. Some of the Antarctic species, however, are known only from the remains of their beaks in predators' stomachs: as many as 18,000 beaks have been found in the stomach of a single sperm whale.

One of the commercially important species of squid is *Martialia hyadesi*, the object of exploratory fishing around South Georgia in 1989.

It is believed that there are large stocks of oceanic squid in the Southern Ocean, for seabirds, seals and whales alone are estimated to consume up to 34 million tonnes a year. Since it requires about three times that amount to support such a loss, a conservative estimate of the total squid stock in the Antarctic seas would be 100 million tonnes. Even such a crude calculation shows that squids are one of the most important components of the food web in the Southern Ocean.

Antarctic fish

Fish are much more accessible to scientists than squids, for most of them live near the surface of the ocean and are much easier to catch. There are about 20,000 species of living fish and of these about 200 are represented south of the Antarctic Polar Front. Because of Antarctica's isolation, up to 85 per cent of its coastal, shallow water fish are restricted to the region. But in deep waters (which are similar all over the world) only 25 per cent of its fish are unique to the Antarctic. Surprisingly, considering the abundant food in the Southern Ocean, there are no densely schooling fish like the herring or capelin of the north.

Bottom-living fish

Like several Antarctic animal groups, the 84 or so species of fish which live near the sea floor have adapted remarkably well to living in a wide variety of habitats. This adaptation points to a burst of evolution, when they diverged rapidly from a few common ancestors.

In Antarctica there are local depressions (of anything up to 1,200 metres deep) in the continental shelf, separated from the continental shelf proper by shallower sills. Since, as we have already seen, the Antarctic continental shelf is unusually deep (commonly 500-750 metres), many typical Antarctic shelf fish are deep water species, and can also be found on the continental slope and in deep trenches. (The greatest depths at which fish have been caught are 4,572 metres in the Weddell Sea and 5,474 metres in the South Orkneys Trench.) These species, which have been little studied, include rat tails, deep sea cod, deep sea eels, snailfish, eel pouts and dragon fishes. Most of them are common and widespread in deep waters, but their geographical distribution in the Southern Ocean is all but unknown.

Resistance to freezing

It is possible for fish to survive with their tissues and fluids in a supercooled state, provided they can avoid contact with ice (which causes immediate freezing). Some fish live in waters deep enough to avoid ice, but other adaptations are necessary to exploit the richer, shallower waters. One way is to produce anti-freeze, which stops them from freezing when cooled to -2°C even when they come into direct contact with ice, by a mechanism which is still not understood.

A bottom-living fish, *Trematomus newnesii* in seaweed off Signy Island.

Metabolic adaptations

The fish found in the high Antarctic latitudes are unable to survive temperatures above 4-6°C, which seems to indicate that their body-controlling enzyme systems have evolved for maximum efficiency under cold water conditions. We know that the rates of chemical reactions are greatly influenced by temperature, as are the enzymes which catalyse them, and that most processes slow down at low temperatures. But while many things do seem to proceed slowly in Antarctic fish, they still feed and move as rapidly as temperate species. Our knowledge at present, though, is very limited, so this could be an exciting area for future research.

A diver with a ghost-like Antarctic icefish, *Chaenocephalus aceratus* which reaches a length of 75 cm.

Bloodless fish

In 1931 it was discovered that some Antarctic fish have colourless blood, due to the absence of haemoglobin, the oxygen-carrying protein which colours other blood red. This gives them a ghostly look and the name icefish. It is only possible because more oxygen dissolves in fluids at lower temperatures. In general the haemoglobin concentration in the blood of Antarctic fish is half that of bony fish found elsewhere, and the red blood cell counts are also half the normal levels.

All the members of the Channichthyidae lack red blood, although their ancestors had it, for they still carry non-functional red blood cells. Their blood is translucent, yellowish (like blood serum) and their gills are white. Oxygen is carried round the body in a simple solution in the plasma instead, which means that the oxygen carrying capacity is only ten per cent of that of other species in the same environment.

Remarkably, this does not make them any less active: but their heart is

The South Georgian cod, *Notothenia rossii*, up to 90 cm long, was the first Antarctic fish species to be overexploited when catches peaked at 400,000 tonnes in 1970/71. Juveniles are inshore bottom feeders, moving offshore as adults to feed on krill.

twice the size and has to work ten times harder (though not faster) than that of a similar sized cod, and they have three to four times as much blood.

Fish of the open ocean

There are no true epipelagic (surface water) fish in the Southern Ocean, and large concentrations of feeding fish are rarely, if ever, found in the open ocean. In this respect the Southern Ocean is very different from the Arctic, which is surprising in view of the abundance of krill.

The deepest-dwelling of Antarctica's open-ocean (pelagic) fish live below the point where light penetrates, and include rat tails, lantern fishes and deep-sea angler fishes. None of them belong solely to the Antarctic, and most are represented by only one or two species.

In the middle depths, however, there are many specifically Antarctic species, among which are a number of formerly deep-water fish which have adapted to living a mid-water life in order to feed on krill.

Growth, age and reproduction

Many fish can be aged by referring to layers in hard structures such as scales and otoliths, and this gives us ages of up to 9-10 years for smaller species and 20-22 years for larger ones. Scales cannot be used for icefish, but fin ray sections indicate maximum ages for three species of icefish of 13-15 years. Growth rates are generally slower than in tropical or temperate species, and the Antarctic fish fauna is dominated by small species, less than half of which exceed 25 centimetres.

Such slow growth rates and long lifespans means that sexual maturity comes much later to Antarctic fish — five to seven years in two main groups, although only two years in the case of icefish. Egg production is relatively low, and ranges from around a hundred to a maximum of about half a million.

In the cold waters of the Southern Ocean one reproductive strategy is to produce just a few large, yolky eggs, resulting in larvae which are more advanced at hatching, enabling them to swim and feed more successfully. Another strategy, is to produce many small eggs on or near the more temperature-stable bottom of the ocean, many of which can afford to be lost. Some species such as Harpagifer actively guard their eggs, which are preyed on by other fish and even the Weddell seal.

Feeding

Many fish groups feed opportunistically, and are often dependent on krill: some 40 surface water species are associated with krill swarms, some of them feeding at night and resting on the bottom during the day. When krill is in short supply some species turn to other fish, or enter the pack ice, where they can prey on the organisms which live there. Because each predator tends to consume its prey at a particular depth or in a particular habitat there is little competition between species except for krill.

opposite
The nest-breeding Antarctic plunderfish, *Harpagifer bispinnis*, with eggs.

ANTARCTIC AND SUB-ANTARCTIC BIRDS

A blue-eyed shag on its nest at Signy Island.

Birds of land and sea

The vast stretches of the ocean and the small extent of ice-free land mean that almost all Antarctic birds are seabirds, and belong to the two best-adapted marine groups — the penguins, and the albatrosses and petrels. The range of their size is enormous, the weight ratio between the giant emperor penguin and the tiny storm petrel over 1,000 to 1. South of the Antarctic Polar Front only 35 species breed; six penguins, six albatrosses, 18 petrels, one shag and four skuas, gulls and terns. Their variety increases in the sub-Antarctic zone, where they are joined by non-sea birds like the South Georgia pipit, teal and pintail, and also by some exotic vagrants like egrets, which have been blown from South America by strong winds.

Although oceans cover 60 per cent of the Earth's surface, only two to three per cent of birds effectively exploit them, probably because of the constraints of breeding on land. They tend to be much larger than land birds and have larger eggs, typically in small clutches of one egg. Egg

formation is a long process, as are incubation, hatching and fledging, occupying up to half a year in the emperor and a year in the king penguin. They are long lived and show deferred sexual or social maturity. Although species are few, populations are usually very large, and gather together in colonies sometimes containing millions of pairs.

While seabirds may be constrained by the shortage of suitable breeding areas, both flightless and flying birds can range very widely at sea, so the distribution of the food resources is generally less of a problem.

Breeding biology

Broad-billed prions in courtship display at the entrance to their breeding burrow.

The basic pattern of breeding, with individual variations, amongst Antarctic birds is as follows. Breeding birds arrive at the colony, courtship ensues, establishing (or re-establishing) the pair-bond which allows nest-building to begin. After copulation the female goes to sea for an intensive feeding period of two to three weeks, which probably aids egg formation. Then,

returning to the nest, the female lays the egg, only to depart again after a short initial incubation shift. After this point incubation is shared between the sexes until hatching time. The chick is brooded in alternating shifts by one parent at a time, while the other feeds at sea. Later both parents feed the chick, which grows rapidly, laying down fat reserves and in most species becoming larger than the adults in the process. The adults then decrease the rate of its feeding and its weight drops until fledging, while muscles develop, the down moults, feathers, wing and leg bones grow.

A brooding chinstrap penguin snowed-in on its nest by a summer snowstorm.

Courtship display of the light-mantled sooty albatross, South Georgia. Aerial courtship displays are also a feature of this species' breeding behaviour.

With few exceptions Antarctic birds are colonial breeders, but some species, like skuas, terns and gulls, and the light-mantled sooty albatross, are solitary, or nest in small groups. The absence of predators means that few birds have to nest on cliffs, in contrast to the Arctic. Where a peaty grassland or enough soil is available some of the smaller species have developed a burrow-nesting habit: among blue and white-chinned petrels and dove prions respectively, on Bird Island in South Georgia, 14, 72, and 103 burrows have been recorded per 100 square metres!

110

Albatrosses depend on luxuriant vegetation for their large nests, so that their southernmost breeding limit coincides with the limit of tussock grass. Most penguins, however, nest on flat ground, which is particularly important for the emperor and king penguins as they move about with the egg resting on the upper surface of their feet.

The climate determines the breeding season, which is two or three weeks earlier in northerly than in southerly populations of the same species. In most species laying is highly synchronous — within three weeks — which relates to the peaks in phytoplankton (December to January) and of zooplankton (March to April) in the upper 50 metres of the sea. This means that peak demand coincides with peak food supplies and there is little variation in laying dates from year to year. Some species, however, spread their laying over a two to three month period, thus spreading the demand over a longer period.

There are, however, five species which breed during the winter months: the emperor and king penguins, the wandering albatross, the grey petrel and the grey-winged petrel.

Grey-headed albatross chicks sit on raised nests, constructed of mud and vegetation.

The emperor penguin is the largest in its group. It breeds under the most extreme environmental conditions of any vertebrate animal and has adopted a correspondingly bizarre way of life. It lays the egg on the fast ice in late summer so that the young can fledge before the onset of winter the following year. At this time the adults must be in a condition to cope with the long fasts

Colonies of emperor penguins raise their young on the sea ice under the ice cliffs of the Brunt Ice Shelf, Weddell Sea.

and terrible climatic conditions of the winter. The eggs are kept off the ice and incubated on the penguins' feet, protected from the cold by a brood pouch. After an incubation period of some 65 days hatching occurs, during the extended period of winter darkness; chicks are then brooded for more than 40 days and fledged at 60 percent of adult weight.

113

During the incubation and brooding fasts the adults lose up to 40 per cent of their body weight and have to survive temperatures below -48°C combined with winds which can exceed 150 kilometres an hour. In order to survive such conditions the emperor has evolved physiological, anatomical and behavioural adaptations. Its critical temperature (the body temperature below which metabolic rates must increase) of -10°C is five degrees lower than that of the king penguin. Its thermal insulation is similar, but its great size gives it a relatively smaller surface area, and it has smaller flippers and bill, all of which reduce heat loss. The flippers, feet and nasal passages also contain heat exchange systems twice as complex as those found in king penguins.

The emperors' most striking behavioural adaptation is 'huddling', which can involve 5,000 birds at densities of ten per square metre. The huddle moves slowly into the wind but no birds are exposed for long at its edges,

King penguins feeding chicks, South Georgia.

because the windward birds continually shuffle back along the flanks and re-enter the huddle from behind. It has been calculated that huddling reduces the theoretical loss of body weight by 50 to 25 percent.

The king penguin, which looks very similar, has a much more complex breeding system. It has been studied in South Georgia, where its eggs are laid in early December; by June the large brown-coated chicks have fledged and reached 90 per cent of their adult weight. Over the winter, feeding becomes sporadic, with fasts of up to three months, but the following spring they are fed regularly and fledge during November and December. The parents are not able to breed again until March, when they produce a much smaller chick, which overwinters and often dies. If it survives it will not fledge until the summer and the parents are prevented from breeding again that year. Thus the king penguins can only average two chicks every three years, while the emperor can bring up a chick every year.

It seems strange that king penguins, living in much milder conditions than emperor penguins, breed less successfully. One possible explanation could be the competition they face for food supplies with the huge South Georgia elephant seal population. But while 93 per cent of king penguins get through their first year, only 19 per cent of emperors survive it.

Food and feeding: seabird diets

The birds of Antarctica feed mainly on crustacea. Ninety per cent of this is provided by krill, and krill makes up 78 per cent of all the food Antarctic birds eat: recent estimates suggest that birds and their other prey eat something like 115 million tonnes of krill every year.

Penguins dominate Antarctic birdlife, and two thirds of their numbers are

Glossy coated Adelie penguins, newly returned from a feeding trip.

made up of Adelie penguins. In the sub-Antarctic, penguins effectively constitute 80 per cent of the bird life, and half of them are macaroni penguins. Most penguin species feed mainly on crustaceans, supplemented in some cases by fish; but the two largest, the emperor and king penguins, also take fish and squids in large quantities.

But birds that feed on surface-water crustaceans during the summer have to find alternative sources of food in winter, when crustaceans move to greater depths or are covered by pack ice. They either switch to a diet of squids or fish, or migrate northwards like the storm petrels, terns, and the black-browed albatross, which overwinters in South African waters. Those species which remain are sustained by squids and fish. Paradoxically, however, it is in the summer when food may be shortest in supply, because of the heavy demands of chick rearing.

Northern giant petrel and chick at nest in tussock grass, South Georgia.

Unlike the other birds, the giant petrels are carrion feeders and opportunists, taking predominantly penguin carrion at South Georgia and Macquarie Island, while the less numerous northern species is more dependent on fur seal carrion during the pupping season in December. The common giant petrel feeds more at sea, however, on living prey. Male giant petrels are larger than females, allowing them to dominate females at carcasses; so males take a larger proportion of carrion, whilst females catch more live prey. Several other seabirds are, like the giant petrel, also well-known ship followers: these are the wandering albatross, the black-browed albatross, the cape pigeon and Wilson's storm petrel.

Feeding ecology and methods

Antarctic seabirds adopt two broad types of feeding methods. Penguins and shags pursuit-dive, while petrels and albatrosses gather their food by surface feeding. Penguins are superbly adapted for pursuit diving, and by being able to explore the depths (in some species down to 250 metres) they more than make up for their inability to fly. Little is known about the way in which penguins catch their prey, for they are usually out of sight to the human observer. But we can make deductions about their feeding from the timing of their dives, as recorded by newly-developed time-depth recorders.

Cape pigeon and chick at nest on a ledge at Signy Island.

119

opposite
An ethereal snow
petrel in flight.

The Adelie and emperor penguins feed mainly in daylight, and observations suggest that two feeding strategies are employed by emperors: shallow dives, exploring the underside of the sea ice, catching krill and ice-associated fish; and deep dives for fish and squids.

Flying birds are much more closely tied to the surface, with possible depth ranges of between 0.1 to 3 metres, and they show a variety of feeding methods. Storm petrels and terns feed by shallow dipping through the surface film to catch individual prey. Prions filter-feed at the surface with their specialised bills, and albatrosses, petrels and diving petrels use shallow surface dives or plunges. Several albatross species have been observed sitting on the surface of the ocean during the day seizing presumably moribund squids, but the bulk of their feeding is probably by surface seizing at night, when they plunge to one metre or so. Activity meters attached to grey-headed albatrosses have shown that they spend 75 per cent of their time away from the nest in flight and 25 per cent on the sea, mostly at night when the food is near the surface.

The wandering albatross takes squids of up to six kilogrammes, but these are probably carrion, possibly eaten by sperm whales, but later rejected. These squids are active, well-armed predators, so how do albatrosses manage to take them at the surface? It seems probable that squids are often present as predators with krill swarms and become available to surface feeding birds when the krill rise to the surface at night. Concentrations of luminescent krill may be visible to seabirds at night, when they are attracted to them and to the associated fish and squid predators.

Diving petrels can penetrate a few metres; but for the most part they sit on the surface and seize prey. Some species detect the prey and pick it up in flight, like Wilson's storm petrel, which patters over the wave tops, using its long legs and webbed feet as a brake so that it can lean forward and seize prey. It rarely sits on the water.

The blue petrel, like the tern, stoops to the prey from some height, but the dove prion has a different method. It hydroplanes on the surface water, head submerged, feet propelling it forwards, its wings outstretched, continuously filtering out small food organisms with its broad deep bill. This bill is fringed with lamellae like the bills of flamingoes or the baleen plates of the whalebone whales. This allows it to capture vast numbers of small zoo-plankton — 41,000 were counted in one 16 gram stomach sample.

Other petrels use the technique of dipping (capturing larger prey while flying over), each species taking its own particular brand of prey. The blue petrel, for example, takes larger organisms than the dove prion.

Birds are probably aware where the prey-concentration 'hotspots' are likely to be. In a recent research cruise very few large flocks of foraging birds were seen, but under each flock the krill was extremely abundant. Once a few birds discover a krill swarm other birds may see them feeding and join them: once there they tend to stay until they are replete. Birds may also use other species to help them detect concentrations of prey. In the eastern

The tiny Wilson's storm petrel dancing over the surface as it feeds.

Weddell Sea I have seen Antarctic petrels following feeding minke whales, concentrating on the slicks where the whales surface.

Foraging ranges and depths

Bird species may share similar breeding seasons, diets and foraging methods and yet be separated ecologically if they have inshore and offshore feeding zones. The inshore feeders are essentially those species in which both parents feed the chick daily, such as the gentoo penguin, the giant petrel, the dove prion and the diving petrel. Amongst offshore feeders, by contrast, each parent feeds the chick no more often than on alternate days.

The distances over which birds forage during the breeding season vary from the relatively small among penguins and pursuit-diving shags (12 kilometres for the blue-eyed shag to 424 kilometres for the king penguin) to much larger among the flying birds. The wandering albatross, which can fly 1,500 kilometres from its nest in search of food, has probably the most extensive breeding season range of any bird.

Penguins, as we have already seen, compensate for their limited horizontal range by diving to great depths (among emperor penguins to 265 metres, king penguins to 235 metres). Only ten per cent of the dives of king and emperor penguins need to be successful in order to meet their energy requirements. On their four to eight-day feeding trips, these two species make from 500 to 1,200 dives, more than half to depths below fifty metres, with only 50 to 120 dives resulting in the capture of prey.

The king penguin is strikingly marked about the head and neck.

Breeding black-browed albatross in flight, with the tussock slopes of Bird Island behind it.

Distribution outside the breeding season

Very little is known about the whereabouts of Antarctic seabirds outside their breeding seasons, as ships rarely enter the Southern Ocean during the winter months. But the bands returned from birds' legs show that they range very widely, even when young: indeed, juvenile albatrosses and petrels may spend several years continuously at sea, repeatedly circling the world. Most species move north in winter, and a few, like Wilson's storm petrel and Antarctic skuas, even migrate across the equator.

Life histories and breeding success

Most seabirds are long-lived compared to land birds. Adult survival rates are high; in petrels, albatrosses and emperor penguins up to 95 per cent annually, but somewhat lower (82-87 per cent) in other penguins. Small petrels can expect to live for 10-15 years, and giant petrels and albatrosses at least 25 years. Wandering albatrosses at South Georgia and snow petrels on Signy Island were still breeding at ages of 35 years, and some wandering albatrosses and emperor penguins may achieve ages of 70-80 years.

It is rare for chicks to fledge from more than half the eggs laid, but the albatrosses and giant petrels have better breeding success than the penguins and the smaller burrowing petrels. Skuas account for many deaths, taking penguin eggs and chicks as well as small petrels. Giant petrels take recently fledged penguins, while leopard and fur seals prey on young birds as they leave the colonies. On islands where rats and cats have been introduced they have also had adverse effects on the smaller petrels: on Marion Island alone it is estimated that wild cats eat nearly half a million petrels annually, and on Kerguelen the number is thought to be 1.2 million.

Breeding success varies from year to year, depending on the weather and the availability of food such as krill. It is also a useful indicator of the effects on birds of large scale exploitation of the krill, squids and fish by man.

The handsome macaroni is the most abundant penguin in the sub-Antarctic.

126

Population changes

Commercial whaling has severely diminished the numbers of whales, which means that some 150 million tonnes of krill formerly eaten by whales have probably become available to the remaining whales and other predators. Three of the commonest Antarctic seabirds (the chinstrap, Adelie and macaroni penguins) have shown increases in their populations. The chinstrap has shown an average annual population increase of 6-10 per cent over a period of more than 30 years in the colonies studied. The macaroni penguins, similarly, showed large increases in numbers (of up to 9 per cent a year) between 1957 and 1977, while Adelie penguin numbers increased by an average of two to three per cent a year between 1947 and 1978.

A mated pair of wandering albatrosses at their large raised nest; the male is in the foreground.

At the same time the king penguin population is known to have grown: on South Georgia there has been a sixfold increase over 33 years, from 12,000 birds in 1946 to nearly 57,000 in 1979. Though king penguins do not, like the other species just mentioned, feed on krill, the squid they feed on do, and may well have increased.

The numbers of the wandering albatross, however, have declined all over the sub-Antarctic; in South Georgia the population seems to have decreased by 19 per cent since the 1960s. These changes are difficult to interpret in detail, but it seems that their general decline may be due to an increased dependence on scavenging around the fishing fleets, with consequent entanglement in fishing gear such as long lines and nets; but this theory is as yet speculative.

Finally, other environmental changes are happening, both natural and man made, which are bound to influence the bird populations. This is nothing new, however. Studies of bird-enriched (ornithogenic) soils are particularly thought-provoking. In the South Shetland Islands, for example, large areas of such soils have been discovered hidden under plant cover, which were abandoned by penguin breeding colonies hundreds or thousands of years ago. The abandoned rookeries are on the south coast of the island group, whereas the present rookeries are on the north coast. This change, for once, can hardly be put down to human interference.

SEALS AND WHALES

The marine mammals of the Antarctic are particularly well adapted species. As a group the Antarctic seals represent at least 60 per cent of the total world population. They are dominated by the crabeater seal, whose numbers in Antarctica probably make up half the total world stock of seals.

When I first saw the Antarctic seals, forty years ago, I remember how our small ship was surrounded by large numbers of whales as it crawled across the vast Southern Ocean. A few years later, as a whaling inspector on a factory ship in the pack ice, I saw my first living blue whale: there, in the presence of the largest and most majestic of all animals, I was overcome by a feeling of awe.

Returning twenty years later, and several times more recently still, I saw on each visit only a handful of large whales. It is salutary to have had such a direct experience of their loss.

Whales seem to have attracted a unique interest and concern about their fate, although very few people have seen them. Because their brain is large and complex, they are said to have an intelligence which rivals that of humans and a complex social life. But though the blue whale brain is six times the weight of the human brain, it is small in relation to its body size, and in many respects quite primitive.

One new theory suggests that such large brains are necessary because whales, like dolphins, probably cannot dream. This theory posits that rapid eye movement (REM) sleep, which is associated with dreaming, clears space in the brain, wiping out useless memories and making space for new ones. Dolphins (and probably large whales) do not have REM sleep.

Nor does observation support the belief that whales and dolphins have a sophisticated social life: in fact their social life is probably no more complex than that of a herd of antelope. Whatever the final truth, however, people continue to be attracted to whales and the Antarctic remains a stronghold

The minke whale, here coming up to blow, is by far the most abundant whale in the Antarctic seas, with a population of about half a million.

for these magnificent animals.

Antarctic whales range over most of the world's oceans, from the tropics to the polar seas. Before whale hunting began to take effect at the beginning of this century, the southern stocks of baleen (filter-feeding) whales were probably about four times as rich as their counterparts in the north. Today, although no species is actually near extinction, almost all whale stocks have been greatly reduced. The exception is the minke whale, which appears to have increased three or four-fold in numbers.

Antarctic seals and fur seals

It is now generally accepted that the pinniped (seal and walrus) families of animals originated about 30 million years ago in the northern hemisphere, and probably crossed through the tropical barrier along the west coast of South America and into the Southern Ocean during a colder period.

The nearest relatives to the Antarctic ice-breeding seals are the monk

131

seals of the tropics; their ancestors were probably the first to enter the Southern Ocean. Evidence as to when this occurred is provided by fossils from Argentina and South Africa, which date from roughly four to five million years ago. This timing would fit in with the cool periods and pack ice expansion that happened about 4.6 to 7 million years ago.

Elephant and fur seals may have been later arrivals, for there is only one species of southern elephant seal and the southern fur seals all belong to the same genus (*Arctocephalus*). The three species of southern sea lions, restricted to South American coasts, to Auckland, Campbell and the Falklands Islands may have arrived even later.

Whatever their origins, seven species of seal are found today in the Southern Ocean, on the shores of the Antarctic continent and on its offshore islands. Their distribution pattern is, like that of many other Antarctic animals, closely linked to latitude, but it also differs between the continuous southern coastline around Antarctica and the much more broken northern one. Together with the whales, seals are the biggest consumers of krill, and they have been studied in some detail.

With three exceptions the breeding populations of seals are confined to the Antarctic itself. Of the exceptions, the first is the elephant seal, which has a total world population of about 750,000, centred on South Georgia,

On a beach in the South Orkney Islands a black-coated pup elephant seal is flanked by its mother and a huge breeding bull.

Sub-adult male Antarctic fur seals haul out in the South Orkney Islands during summer.

Kerguelen and Macquarie Islands. Elephant seals are also found, in fewer numbers, on the Falkland Islands and along the coast of South America. Since 1951 the population of elephant seals in the Indian Ocean has dropped each year by roughly five per cent, while South Georgia's 102,000 breeding female population seems to have remained static since 1951.

The second species whose breeding is not confined to Antarctica is the fur seal, which has its main colonies in South Georgia, where their numbers in 1988 were approaching two million. The third species, the sub-Antarctic fur seal, is only occasionally seen south of the Antarctic Polar Front. The fur seals are the only two Antarctic examples of the group of seals with external ears. They also swim, unlike true seals, with their large fore-flippers, and have two coats (a dense underfur and a coat of long guard hairs). They were brought, like the elephant seal, near to extinction in the nineteenth century by commercial sealing.

The four truly Antarctic species, almost completely restricted to the pack and fast-ice, are the crabeater, the leopard, the Ross and the Weddell seals. All of them are spotted, blotched or striped, silvery-grey when newly moulted and brown later in the year. The crabeater and leopard seals share similar areas of the pack-ice zone, most of them living around its fringes, but the leopard seal is also found on sub-Antarctic islands and in even lower latitudes. The Ross and Weddell seals are usually seen in the denser parts of the pack ice, though the latter spreads much further south, and also breeds along the coasts of the Antarctic islands. The Weddell seal's most northerly breeding population is a very small relict one at Larsen Harbour in South Georgia where, unusually, pupping takes place on land because the sea rarely freezes so far north.

But it is the crabeater seal which is predominant in Antarctica. The most populous seal on Earth, it is also probably the most numerous large mammal, with a total population estimated at between 15 to 30 million. The uncertainty reflects the extreme difficulty of conducting a census in the vast pack ice zone, an area which varies between 4 and 20 million square kilometres, much of which is virtually inaccessible to ships.

A sight very rarely observed – a female leopard seal and her recently-born pup.

The leopard seal population, like that of Ross seals, is thought to be in the region of 220,000, while Weddell seals are estimated to number around 800,000. The ice-breeding seals all have preferences for particular ice conditions: crabeater and leopard seals, for instance, like small floes in dense pack ice, while Weddell seals frequent much larger floes. Ross seals, however, seem happy on either.

Leopard seal on
floe in characteristic
alert posture.

Outside the breeding season it is not at all clear where several of these
species go. Almost nothing is known about the whereabouts of adult fur
seals, for example, when they are away from their breeding colonies
between May and October. The elephant seal is found up to 2,400
kilometres away from its colonies when not breeding, travelling as far as
South Africa, Tasmania, New Zealand and Mauritius.

Crabeater seal underwater; the multi-lobed teeth, unique among mammals, are designed for straining krill.

Breeding behaviour and reproduction

It is interesting to compare the breeding behaviour of the different Antarctic seals, whose pupping occurs at very restricted periods during the spring. On South Georgia, over 80 per cent of elephant seals are born between 6 and 26 October. Monogamous pack-ice breeders like the crabeater, leopard and Ross seals occupy one end of the behaviour spectrum: their habitat contrasts with the stable ice-platform occupied by the female Weddell seal during the breeding season. This more stable habitat has made the development of gregarious pupping colonies possible, where dominant males display and defend three-dimensional territories in the water beneath and mate with entering females.

The polygynous (having more than one female partner) mating behaviour of the Weddell seal stands half way between the monogamous pattern of the crabeater, leopard and Ross seals and the highly polygynous mating system of the land-breeding elephant and fur seals. While the females of all the ice-breeding seals are larger than the males, among the land-breeding fur seals males reach 4-5 times the size, and male elephant seals can be 8-10 times the size of their females.

The Weddell seal has evolved to make full use of the stable fast-ice close to the shores of the continent and around its offlying islands, where it establishes pupping colonies and winters under the ice, keeping breathing holes open with its teeth. Between September and November, female Weddell seals haul themselves out onto the surface of the ice along tide cracks (whose position is predictable from year to year), in order to give birth and suckle the pup for five to six weeks. Shortly before the pup is weaned the females come into heat and mating takes place under the ice.

Weddell seal at breathing/haul-out hole in spring.

Female Weddell seal with her young pup.

Crabeater seals give birth on drifting ice floes during the austral (southern hemisphere) spring. Each cow and pup pair is then joined by an adult male, forming a characteristic breeding group, usually separated from other crabeaters by a kilometre or more of pack ice. The suckling period is no more than four weeks, probably less. During this period the pup grows remarkably fast, from about 26 kilogrammes at birth to 110 kilogrammes at weaning. As suckling progresses the male becomes more and more pressing in his attentions to the female, who initially repulses him. But by the time a pup is a month old its mother is back on heat and mating, probably in the water. From this point onwards the pup has no more contact with its mother and takes to the water. There it is immediately preyed upon by leopard seals, often before it has even learned to swim properly — a disastrous entry into the world.

The leopard seals breed later, and the cow and pup pair is not joined by a male. Mating also takes place after, rather than before, the pup becomes fully independent. Like the others, this largest of all the ice-breeding Antarctic seals probably mates in the water.

Very little is known about the Ross seal, but pupping occurs in November and December. Its mating behaviour is thought to be similar to that of the leopard seal, for males have not been seen in attendance on the cows and pups.

Elephant seals give birth in September or October, fur seals between November and December. These two species prefer different types of breeding sites (large open beaches for elephant seals, rocky shores and small, sheltered beaches for fur seals), which minimises competition between them. Both species have a highly developed polygynous social organisation, in which dominant males prevent subordinate males from approaching the breeding females. While elephant seal pups quadruple in weight during the 23-day suckling period, the females fast and lose some 300 kilogrammes. In contrast, the female fur seal makes frequent feeding trips to sea during the 110 to 120 days she provides the pup with milk.

In summer crabeater seals lie out on small floes usually in twos and threes.

Life histories and causes of death

The age of seals can be determined by looking at the annual growth layers in their teeth, and reveals that longevity ranges from 20 years in the elephant seal to 40 years or more in the crabeater. These growth layers also record the reproductive history of each individual seal. Combining age, length and weight enables growth rates to be determined: amongst the polygynous, harem-breeding species, for instance, the male grows larger than the female due to a pubertal growth spurt. As a result the fully adult Antarctic fur seal is on average 4 ½ times the weight of the adult female, and the male elephant seal is eight times heavier. This is the reverse of the ice-breeding seals, where females are larger than males.

The lives of crabeater seals are affected by two predators. Leopard seals kill many of their young, but they generally outlast Weddell seals if they survive the first year of their life, reaching ages of forty years. Eighty per cent of adult crabeater seals bear parallel leopard-seal scars on their bodies. Fresh wounds are virtually restricted to young pups between six months and a year old. Presumably younger pups do not survive encounters with leopard seals, but as they gain in experience their chances of escape improve. The killer whale takes crabeaters of all ages, often hunting in organised packs. This pressure from predators is thought to have played a major role in the evolution of the crabeater's breeding behaviour.

By contrast, the Weddell seal's fast-ice habitat both reduces the pressure of predation on its young and allows it to exploit inshore prey all year round. But this way of life also has its drawbacks. Most Weddell seals living on fast-ice have worn incisor teeth, which are used to saw through the ice to open and maintain their breathing and access holes. This wear increases with age, so that by the time they are eight to ten years old the teeth are worn down far enough to expose the pulp, leading to infections and abscesses. In older animals this prevents them keeping their breathing holes in the ice open, and leads to their deaths. As a result few Weddell seals live beyond 20 years.

Food and feeding

Like other groups of Antarctic animals, seals have adopted many different feeding habitats. Of the two seals common in ice-free waters, the elephant seal appears to eat approximately 75 per cent squid and 25 per cent fish; the fur seal, however, feeds almost exclusively on krill during breeding, and fish and squids during winter. Among the ice-breeding seals, the diet of Weddell seals seems to favour fish; crabeater seals eat mainly krill, and leopard seals a mixture of krill and birds, other seals and carrion. Ross seals appear to prefer squid. The leopard seal diet apparently varies with age and the time of year, younger animals taking a higher proportion of krill, while for the adult leopard seals, young crabeaters are an important food source in early summer.

opposite
Weddell seal under inshore fast ice.

Thin longitudinal section of a crabeater seal postcanine tooth, showing the multi-lobed crown and annual layers in dentine (next to pulp cavity) and in the cement (deposited on the outside of the tooth).

All Antarctic seals fast for greater or lesser periods during the breeding season, with the elephant seal also fasting (up to 50 days among males and 32 among females) during their moulting period. Taken together, all these different mechanisms (distribution, feeding behaviour, diving adaptations and breeding behaviour) separate the various seal populations from one another and allow them to coexist successfully.

Changing population sizes

The population of Antarctic fur seals at South Georgia, in its protected recovery from earlier over-hunting, has increased from a few hundred in the 1950s to around two million today. Such an accelerated recovery is thought, however, only to have been enabled by the increased availability of krill since whale numbers were greatly reduced.

With a population estimated at 15-30 million the crabeater is by far the most abundant seal in the world.

Antarctic fur seals breeding colony on a beach at South Georgia, backed by tussock-covered slopes. The population currently numbers about two million and is increasing.

The crabeater seals also appear to be increasing in number, again probably as a result of the greatly reduced competition from whales for food. The stocks of Antarctic seals may now total as many as 33 million, annually consuming around 130 million tonnes of krill (2-3 times the current estimates of its consumption by whales), as well as ten million tonnes of squid and at least eight million tonnes of fish. But their role in the Southern Ocean ecosystem, and what they can tell us about natural and man-made changes there, are questions which remain to be answered.

Antarctic whales and dolphins

Whales (of which there are two types, toothed and baleen), unlike seals, are confined entirely to the sea, only breaking the surface to breathe or occasionally to make a spectacular leap (or breach). This, added to their great range, makes them much more difficult to study, and it may be this mystery which lies at the heart of the unique sympathy we feel for them.

Most baleen (filter feeding) whales go on long seasonal migrations between the tropical or subtropical breeding areas where they winter, and the polar feeding grounds which are uncovered by the contracting pack-ice belt during summer. The migrations of the humpback whale are best known of these journeys, because they pass so close to coasts. Adult male sperm whales also migrate into polar waters, but females rarely, if ever, enter the Southern Ocean. The numbers of male sperm and whalebone whales in the Southern Ocean reach a peak between January and March, but they are very scarce during the winter.

Dolphins and the other small toothed cetaceans (whales), on the other hand, do not appear to undertake proper migrations, and many of them are unknown north of the Polar Front.

The large baleen whales of the Southern Ocean fall into six species and one subspecies. In addition to the huge blue whale (up to 30 metres long and 150 tonnes in weight) and its smaller subspecies the pygmy blue, these are the fin (25 metres, 90 tonnes), sei (18 metres, 30 tonnes), minke (11 metres, 19 tonnes), the much plumper, long-flippered humpback (16 metres, 60 tonnes), and the southern right whale (at 18 metres and 90 tonnes, even plumper than the humpback).

There is one large toothed whale, the sperm whale, the average male of which measures 18 metres and weighs 70 tonnes, and the female 11 metres and 17 tonnes. Eleven other smaller toothed whales are found in the Antarctic proper, led by that important predator on seals, the killer whale (male nine metres, eight tonnes and female slightly smaller). Among the colourful dolphins is the beautifully patterned southern white-sided dolphin. There is a southern bottle-nosed dolphin, plus two beaked-whale species. Knowledge of these small toothed whales is still very superficial and often comes not from observations of living dolphins, or planned scientific sampling, but from the examination of stranded specimens.

Reproduction

The reproductive cycle of baleen whales is closely tied to the extreme seasonality of the Antarctic environment and their long-range migrations between breeding and feeding areas. Mating, and birth, occurs in the tropics or sub-tropics, with gestation periods of less than a year. The growth of baleen whale embryos is unique among mammals, not only because of its magnitude — a blue whale calf weighs 2½ tonnes at birth — but because of

A fin whale blowing on the Antarctic feeding grounds; formerly a preferred target of the whaling industry there are now about 70,000 left.

its unusual growth rate. Like other mammals, the embryo of the baleen whales grows initially at a steady rate, but then it begins to grow exponentially. Because of this exponential growth even a slight lengthening of the gestation period would result in the calf becoming unmanageably large for the mother's body. Interestingly this marked change in the rate of foetal growth corresponds to the time when whales begin actively feeding on krill in the Southern Ocean.

After birth, most baleen whales spend six to seven months feeding the young, weaning the calf shortly after entering the Antarctic waters. The reproductive cycle varies between two to three years according to species, but there is evidence of an increase in the pregnancy rates, probably related to the decreased numbers of whales and the resultant increase in available krill. The sei whale has shown a similar change since 1945.

Female sperm whales do not migrate to the Antarctic, and so are not so rigidly tied to an annual cycle as the baleen whales. Their foetal growth remains linear, but they still produce large calves by extending their

gestation period to 15 months; they then suckle for several years. What evidence there is about the effects of commercial whaling on sperm whales is conflicting, but one would expect earlier sexual maturity and increased pregnancy rates amongst a reduced female population, or a reduction of pregnancy rates if too few males survive.

Unlike the baleen whales, which are monogamous, the sperm whale has a breeding system which used to be compared to a harem. Now, however, it is known that the 'harem' is really a family group of sperm whale cows together with their daughters of all ages and their younger male offspring (males are expelled from the group at puberty). Wandering males seek out family groups looking for females in breeding condition, but do not stay long with the females.

On average male social maturity is deferred until the age of 26 years, by which time their physical growth is almost complete. This breeding system is remarkably similar to that of the African elephant, studies of which can throw light on sperm whale behaviour.

Growth and age

Like seals, annual growth rings in the teeth of toothed whales can be used to determine their age, but baleen whales have to be aged by the annual layers in their wax earplugs. Transitional zones in such plugs have been interpreted to give controversial evidence of a general decline in the age at which sexual maturity is reached. Such evidence seems to show that, as commercial whaling has reduced whale stocks, so whales have been growing faster and maturing earlier. For example, the 1930 fin whale year-class reached a length of 20 metres in ten years, but today they would reach that in six.

In the baleen whale, females reach larger sizes than males, but the sperm whale shows a more marked sexual dimorphism (size and shape differences between the sexes) in favour of the male.

Migrations and distribution

The whalebone whales migrate into Antarctic waters in summer to feed. The geographical distribution of commercial catches seems to show that there are separate feeding stocks, most distinct among humpbacks, but also recognisable among blue and fin whales. The position is less clear in the case of sei and minke whales.

Migrations are staggered, with the largest species tending to arrive the earliest in Antarctic waters. First comes the blue whale, followed by the fin and humpback whales, then the sei. Such waves of migration also reflect the extent to which different species penetrate into colder waters and this is also correlated with body size (the minke being a notable exception). As a result, although the Antarctic distributions of the different species overlap, each occupies a distinct latitudinal zone. The blue and minke whales feed in the extreme south, often close to or among the drifting pack ice. The next largest, the fin and humpback whales, tend to feed further north, and the sei more northerly still. At the southern extreme only the blue, minke, killer and beaked whales significantly penetrate into the pack-ice zone.

Right whales, formerly grossly over-hunted, feed furthest north of all, although they are being seen around South Georgia in increasing numbers. Off South African coasts, aerial surveys indicate that their numbers have been recovering over a long period by a fairly steady annual rate of about seven per cent. Recent counts off the northeast coast of Australia have shown that humpback whales there have been increasing by around 13 per cent a year, which is around the maximum theoretical rate of increase for the species.

There are also longitudinal variations in number both within and between species, almost certainly related to the distribution and abundance of their food resources around the polar feeding grounds. Larger and older whales also tend to enter colder waters earlier in the season. Pregnant females arrive early and leave late, and females with calves postpone their entry into polar waters until near weaning, allowing the calf time to lay down a protective layer of insulating blubber.

Animals which remain too long in their summer range may become trapped by consolidating and freezing pack ice or by the direct formation of fast-ice. They are then confined to small pools of open water, kept open by their surfacing to blow. Thirty years ago just such a pool was found being shared by minke whales, killer whales, and crabeater, leopard and Weddell seals. The phenomenon is reported more frequently in the Arctic, where it is well known to the Inuit (Eskimos). In October 1988 three gray whales were trapped in this way off Alaska, arousing great public interest.

Food and feeding behaviour

Blue, fin, sei, minke and humpback whales are all seen singly or in small groups of three to five individuals, but crowds of up to 100 minke whales have been reported diving in unison. The right whales usually gather in groups of no more than six, possibly family units. Krill forms the major food of all baleen whales, but the more northerly species (right and some sei whales) feed mainly on copepods.

The feeding apparatuses of the whalebone whales — mouth and baleen plates — are functionally adapted to the size of their food. The blue whale has coarse bristle filters, the fin whale has finer ones, while the sei and right whales have very fine bristles (to cope with copepods). The humpback's apparatus comes somewhere in-between.

Baleen whales feed in three different ways. In the first, a mouthful of water and food is gulped as the throat grooves are distended. Then the tongue is raised to expel the water through the baleen filter, netting the organisms inside. How they are then transferred to the stomach is still unclear. The humpbacks will first circle a swarm of krill and rise vertically with their mouths open to engulf their prey; a variant is to swim in an ascending spiral around the swarm, releasing bubbles which rise to the surface and form a 'bubble net', through which they swim upwards.

The second feeding method, skimming, is a more continuous process of filtering, which involves swimming along with the jaws slightly open. This method is typical of the right whale. The third involves the use of both previous methods practised for example by the sei whale.

The sperm whale feeds mainly on the smaller squids, but it also takes fish. How they hunt in the black waters at great depths (they can dive to 3,000 metres) is a mystery but probably involves echo-location. One theory suggests that they stun their prey using an intense beam of directional sound.

The diet of the smaller toothed whales is little known, but is presumed to contain mostly small squids and fish. The killer whale, however, is an opportunistic feeder, taking squids and fish, but also preying on seals and other whales. They usually go around in small 'pods' of between five and ten animals, possibly a family group or an extended family, but large groups of

Spy-hopping, a
typical behaviour
pattern of the
predatory killer
whale.

over 100 have also been observed. Like the Arctic wolf or the African
hunting dog it is a cooperative hunter. In the pack ice it has sometimes been
seen hunting seals basking on floes. Having sighted the seal, the pod of killer
whales swims a little way off, then turns and swims at the surface as a group
towards the floe. As they approach the floe they turn broadside on, creating a
large wave which may wash the seal off the floe. Once in the water it is
accessible to the killers.

An even more unusual predatory pattern has been filmed on the coast of
Patagonia, where there are breeding colonies of the southern sea lion. Here,
killer whales regularly take sea lions in the surf zone, but they even attack
some of them on land. If a sea lion is close to the water's edge a killer whale
may swim up to it and seize it, temporarily beaching itself in the process.

Changes in numbers due to commercial exploitation

The Antarctic baleen whales and the sperm whales have been hunted since
1904. At this time their numbers are estimated to have been about 1.1
million. Since 1920, statistics record that a huge total of 1.3 million whales

have been killed. Commercial catches of blue and humpback whales ended in the 1960s, and of fin and sei whales during the 1970s, but continued until 1986/7 for minke whales. Population estimates for whales are very difficult, because of their remoteness and the limited time they spend at the surface of the ocean.

Four methods have been used to estimate the sizes of whale populations, and to study their structures and biology: catch-per-unit-effort, mark-recapture analysis, earplug ageing and whale sighting cruises. New methods are being developed, based on individual recognition from colour patterns, notches and scars, and from DNA fingerprinting (requiring a small tissue sample from living whales), from photography, and from the 'sonar clicks' of sperm whales. These studies, though promising, are in their infancy and it is difficult to see how they can be successfully applied to the more abundant species of whales in the open ocean.

The best estimates of current Antarctic stocks of whalebone whales are; right whales, 3,000; blue, 8,000; sei, 30,000; humpback, 40,000; fin, 70,000; and minke 565,000. No species is near extinction, though the right and blue whale populations are uncomfortably small.

Before the Antarctic whale fishery began the total biomass of Antarctica's stock of whales was about 45 million tonnes, and they consumed each year an estimated 190 million tonnes of krill, 14 million tonnes of squid and nearly five million tonnes of fish. Competition for the available food probably limited their sizes and numbers.

By 1973, over-hunting had drastically reduced their numbers to about 500,000, with a biomass of nine million tonnes, and their annual intake had fallen to about 43 million tonnes of krill, six million tonnes of squid and only 130,000 tonnes of fish. So the whaling industry has caused a major disruption of the Antarctic marine ecosystem, changing the abundance of krill, squid and fish, and increasing the numbers of higher predators, such as birds, seals and minke whales.

How did this situation come about? The history of whaling in the Antarctic is of the progressive depletion of species, starting with the humpback (which was the easiest to catch), then the blue whale (the largest and most valuable). As blue whales declined in numbers and became more difficult to catch, the industry switched to the smaller fin whales, then to sei and finally to minke. Very few sperm whales were caught until the mid 1940s, and the subsequent annual catches rarely exceeded 5,000. The species has been protected since 1978.

Only 2,000 minke whales were taken before the 1970s, but since 1975 it has been the main catch, because blue, fin, sei and humpback whales have been protected. Because of the reduced competition for krill, minke whale numbers may have increased to higher levels than the original population. However, despite the increased growth rates and the accelerated sexual maturity already examined, these larger numbers could partly be the result of improved estimates.

Whalers' graves at
Signy Island, South
Orkney Islands,
dating from the
shore whaling
station 1921-26.

MAN AND THE ANTARCTIC

Sea fog and climber
– the Breccia crags,
Coronation Island.

Arrival on the scene

The Antarctic is the most remote region on Earth, subject to the most extreme climate and surrounded by a vast, deep and stormy ocean. Until recently it was completely unpopulated, and the nearest people were the relatively primitive tribes who inhabited the other southern continents. While both the Maoris of New Zealand and the Alacaluf indians of Tierra del Fuego probably could have ventured south, either on planned journeys or by being blown off course, the odds would be greatly against their survival. And so, unlike any other continent in the world, the Antarctic has

no human population.

Around 500BC the ancient Greek philosophers named the night sky's brightest constellation *Arctos* (the bear), and the point about which it appears to turn the Arctic pole. To satisfy their sense of symmetry an opposite pole was logically required in the southern hemisphere; an anti-Arctic pole. During the Elizabethan period geographers like Mercator came up with the idea that a hypothetical southern continent was needed to balance the globe's northern land masses. A typical sixteenth century world map, published in 1531, shows a vast continent centred on the South Pole, filling most of the Southern Ocean and with Tierra del Fuego as its northern tip.

The first authenticated discovery of land south of the Polar Front was in April 1675, by a London merchant called Antoine de la Roche. Winds and currents swept his ship off course near the tip of South America and it appears that he anchored in Drygalski Fjord at the southern end of South Georgia. In 1739 a Frenchman, Bouvet de Lozier, discovered a small island (now named after him) and described icebergs and penguins in the Southern Ocean. The next record comes from June 1756, when the 486 ton ship Leon was blown east off Cape Horn and sighted Annenkov Island and South Georgia, reporting many birds, seals and whales.

These reports of land and of icebergs led geographers to return to the Elizabethan theory about a huge southern continent, which they imagined to have great riches, and in 1772 two expeditions set sail, one from Britain and one from France. The French party was led by Yves de Kerguelen, who was unable to land on the island now named after him because of fog and ice conditions. Undeterred, he fabricated rather optimistic descriptions of a land of opportunity, where wood, minerals, diamonds and rubies would be found. Unfortunately, his second expedition revealed the sorry truth, and for a time it was known as the Land of Desolation.

Amundsen-Scott Station at the South Pole, with flags of the Antarctic Treaty nations.

The other expedition, sent out by the British Admiralty, was led by Captain James Cook. On his second, three-year-long voyage, the principal objective of which was to investigate the 'Southern Continent', he made many important discoveries. Cook's party set out in June 1772 in HMS Resolution (462 tons) and HMS Adventure (336 tons), two Whitby-built colliers which had been refitted as naval sloops. The expedition was the first to cross the Antarctic Circle and to dispel the myth of a rich and temperate Terra Australis.

In 1773/74 he attempted to penetrate the pack ice, reaching latitude 71°10′S near Byrd Land, but did not see the continent. In January 1775 Cook rediscovered South Georgia, landing to claim possession. This was the first claim to sovereignty in the Antarctic made by any nation, and they named the bay where they landed Possession Bay. Cook named and described a number of other features as far as the southernmost tip, which he later named Cape Disappointment, because it was at this point that he realised that South Georgia was an island and not part of the great southern continent.

The voyage took place during the 'Little Ice Age', which was at its peak around 1700, when global temperatures were perhaps 1.5°C lower than at present. So South Georgia was more ice-bound and glaciated than it is today, and Cook described it and the South Sandwich Islands as 'Lands doomed by Nature to perpetual frigidness: never to feel the warmth of the sun's rays; whose horrible and savage aspects I have not words to describe'.

These gloomy early reports were hardly encouraging, revealing as they did lands which were remote, inhospitable, and barren. Even its seals were more numerous and could be hunted more easily elsewhere, as could the whales. Sealing and whaling were well established industries, and sealers were continually searching for new sealing grounds, as they hunted population after population to near extinction. Because of this they were usually among the first arrivals to newly discovered areas where seals were reported. Consequently, Cook's detailed accounts were taken up by British and American sealers, who operated from South Georgia from 1784 onwards. By 1830 they had brought the seals near extinction.

But though the sealers were the first to explore south of South Georgia to the Antarctic Peninsula their activities led to little increase in knowledge. As competitive businesses they were secretive, making none of their reports public, producing no maps and carrying few if any scientists. As a result, the first *recorded* sightings of the Antarctic continent were made, all in 1820, by three countries: Britain, Russia and the United States. The Russian Admiral, von Bellingshausen, probably sighted it in January or February, though he made no claims. Edward Bransfield, a British naval officer, sighted the Antarctic Peninsula in February. And an American sealing captain, Nathaniel Palmer, claimed a sighting in November. The first recorded landing on the continent was made early in 1821 by Captain John Davis of the American sealer Huron, on the Antarctic Peninsula.

A series of government-supported voyages followed, charting coastlines and adding a great deal to knowledge of the region. Of the British expeditions, the one led by James Clark Ross between 1839 and 1843 to the other side of the Continent was the best-prepared and most successful up to that time. Ross had over 18 years of previous experience in Arctic exploration, two well-founded ships, and hand-picked officers and men, many of them also with former Arctic experience.

None of these expeditions set foot on the continent, but their findings helped the planning of later expeditions in the 'heroic age' of exploration which followed.

The 'heroic age': the beginnings

In 1895 the so-called 'heroic age' was launched with the resolution, at the Sixth International Geographic Congress in London, that 'the exploration of the Antarctic region is the greatest piece of geographical exploration still to be undertaken'. The enormous international interest that followed led to a substantial increase in knowledge, but at the expense of great suffering — exposure, frostbite, scurvy and death.

The first of these great expeditions began in 1897 when the Belgian De Gerlache made frequent landings on the west side of the Antarctic Peninsula. Among the ship's complement were Amundsen, F.A. Cook, Arctowski and Racovitza, some of whom later became famous in polar exploration. The ship froze into the pack ice in March 1898 and drifted during the long polar night for 347 days in the pack ice of the Bellingshausen Sea, thus becoming the first recorded expedition to winter in Antarctica. (However, archaeological remains on the South Shetland Islands, and the practices adopted by sealing parties suggest that they had probably wintered earlier.)

Hard after this came the first expedition to winter on land, at Cape Adare in Victoria Land (1898-1900), led by the Norwegian, Borchgrevinck. One of his scientists died and became the first person to be buried in Antarctica. An official German expedition in the specially-built polar ship Gauss was the first to document the abrupt sinking of the cold Antarctic Surface Water at the Polar Front, in 1901-03. Later the ship was trapped in pack ice for a year. During the same period the Swede, Nordenskjold, with C.A. Larsen as Captain of the *Antarctic*, had a particularly exciting time: parties wintered on islands off the Antarctic Peninsula, then the ship was crushed in the pack ice and sank, leaving them to pass a second winter until rescued by the Argentine Navy.

The seige of the South Pole

For all their solid scientific achievements, what all these previous expeditions lacked was the romance and excitement of the races to the North and

South Poles, which came to grip the popular imagination at the beginning of the new century. Between 1901 and 1912 the scene was dominated by the expeditions of Scott, Shackleton and Amundsen and the south magnetic pole was attained.

Amundsen, a late arrival on the scene and new to Greater Antarctica, reached the pole first using dogs, on 14 December 1911. Scott's team finally reached it a month later, on 18 January 1912, having manhauled all the way. On the return journey, exhausted by their exertions, delayed by bad weather and with dwindling supplies, Scott and his companions died only 18 kilometres from a depot of supplies that would have ensured their safe return. Ironically it is the glorious failure and ultimate demise of Scott's party which tends to be remembered, rather than the success and efficient methods of Amundsen. So ended the quest for the South Pole.

But this was not the end of the heroic age, for an even more ambitious goal remained — the crossing of Antarctica via the pole. Several explorers entertained the idea, but it was Shackleton who made the attempt in 1914-16. He aimed to cross the continent from the Weddell to the Ross Sea, but his ship was trapped and eventually crushed in the pack ice. After great tribulations drifting in the pack the party came to open water and crossed to Elephant Island in the ship's boats. While one group remained on the beach at Elephant Island, Shackleton undertook a remarkable small-boat journey to South Georgia, 1,300 kilometres away, and then crossed the unknown centre of the island from south to north coasts, all in appalling conditions and with makeshift equipment. After several abortive attempts the party on Elephant Island was rescued by a Chilean vessel. Although the expedition had failed it provided a classic story of leadership which still inspires people today. It was not until more than forty years later that the crossing was finally achieved by Fuchs.

Even into the present century Antarctic expeditions continued to retain a strong nineteenth-century feeling, thanks to the persistence of earlier values and social distinctions. These were particularly strong on voyages led by naval officers such as Scott, with sharp distinctions between officers and other ranks. It was the First World War that brought such distinctions to an end, while the popular interest that had attended the expeditions of the heroic age dwindled after the pole itself was reached.

Territorial claims and the first aerial explorations

The First World War also saw governments beginning to show an interest in Antarctic territory. First came Britain, which in 1908 made a formal claim centred on the Antarctic Peninsula and the Weddell Sea, which was renewed in 1917. It was followed by claims, in 1923 and 1933, to what is now the Ross Dependency (by New Zealand) and Australian Antarctic Territory. France claimed Adelie Land in 1924, Argentina made a claim which overlapped the British one in the Antarctic Peninsula in 1925, and in

1939 Norway claimed Dronning Maud Land. During World War II Argentina renewed its claim and Chile made its first claim (in 1940), which overlapped both the British and Argentine claims. The United States, although it was expected to claim the Pacific Sector — tacitly left unclaimed — made no territorial claims and reserved its position on sovereignty, a policy later adopted by the Soviet Union. These claims to sovereignty were to have a major influence on later developments, particularly during the period of the 'Cold War' that followed World War II.

The introduction of aircraft into the Antarctic transformed the possibilities for polar exploration, though in the early days planes were unreliable, making polar flying particularly hazardous, since there was little chance of rescue should a plane crash in a remote region. On the other hand, a plane could survey thousands of square kilometres an hour — equivalent to a whole season's work with dog teams.

A persistent footprint in moss turf on Signy Island such prints may remain for decades.

163

TERRITORIAL CLAIMS

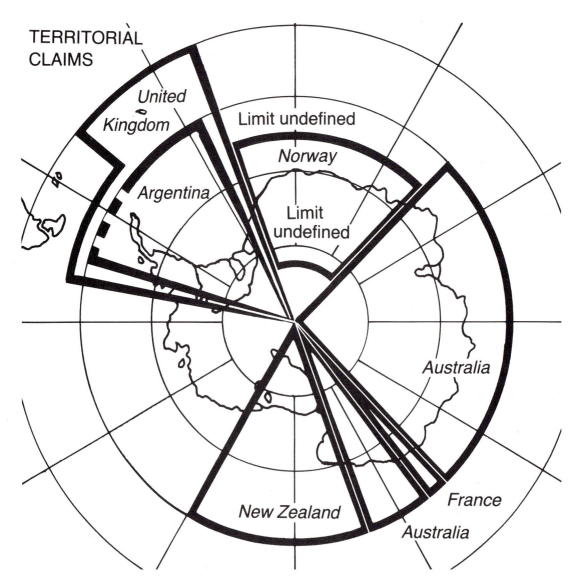

Seven nations have made territorial claims to sovereignty over the Antarctic; there is an unclaimed region in the Pacific sector and the southern limit of Norway's claim is undefined.

In 1928 Hubert Wilkins made the first flight in the Antarctic, attempting to cross the continent. A further attempt in 1930 was also unsuccessful, but his aerial photographs seemed to show that the Peninsula was separated from the continent by several channels at sea level (this was disproved by the British Grahamland Expedition in 1934–37). The previous year, 1929, the famous American pilot Byrd had flown over the South Pole, and another American, Ellsworth, made the first successful trans-Antarctic flight in 1935. Although Ellsworth claimed the Pacific Sector for the USA the American government did not follow it up. In 1938-39 the German, Ritscher, led an expedition which symbolically staked a claim to Dronning Maud Land by dropping thousands of metal darts engraved with Nazi swastikas.

A significant motivation behind many expeditions right up to the Second World War was simply the spirit of adventure. Many of them had a large measure of private funding, and often the book about the expedition and public lectures were a means of clearing debts incurred, placing a considerable burden particularly on the leader. The vast majority of subsequent exploration has been funded by governments, usually for political reasons (although the spirit of adventure continues to be important).

Antarctic whaling and related research

It was a Norwegian, C.A. Larsen, who first saw Antarctica's potential for the whaling industry. In 1904, having attempted to raise capital elsewhere, he had the first Antarctic whaling station built at Grytviken, South Georgia, funded by Argentine businessmen. It was the start of a major international industry with, in its heyday, a turnover of hundreds of millions of dollars a year. At a very early stage the British government realised that controls would be essential to prevent the whales from being wiped out. Accordingly, in 1904, an ordinance to regulate the whale fishery was implemented by the Governor of the Falkland Islands, and this became the first legal instrument of Antarctic conservation.

A twin Otter aircraft of British Antarctic Survey, fitted for aeromagnetic survey, at a field camp.

Whaling spread to the South Orkneys and Shetlands, where there were good harbours for processing whale carcasses. Later, in 1925, the first whaling factory (with a slipway allowing whale carcasses to be worked up on deck) allowed the industry to exploit whales on the high seas, out of reach of national jurisdiction.

An early colour photograph of Grytviken whaling station, South Georgia at the height of the 1950/51 whaling season; a whale is being dismembered on the plan; others are floating nearby and whale catchers are getting ready for sea.

    The setting up of the British Inter-departmental Committee on Research and Development in the Dependencies of the Falkland Islands, for all its cumbersome title, was a significant development in the history of the Antarctic. The Committee's report, published in 1920, called for detailed scientific studies on whale biology, and followed up an earlier idea that

Two derelict whale catchers, *Diaz* and *Albatros* alongside the abandoned Grytviken station in 1982. I sailed in *Albatros* in 1950 and 1951 when she was used as a sealer.

research ships should be acquired, and paid for by an extra tax on whale products. In 1925 the field programme, which came to be known as the Discovery Investigations, began.

The programme continued into the 1950s, and transformed knowledge of whale biology. A shore station on South Georgia was occupied for six years, observing dead whales at Grytviken whaling station nearby, and three research ships were commissioned. These ships made a series of all-year-round cruises throughout the Southern Ocean until the outbreak of war in 1939. In addition to direct research on whale biology was a programme of work on physical and chemical oceanography, phytoplankton, krill and other zooplankton, fish, birds and seals. The high quality of the Discovery Collections of specimens and data is a continuing basis for a series of monographs centred on the Southern Ocean, which started in 1929 and had produced 38 large volumes by 1988. The costs, as recommended in 1920, were met completely by a tax on each barrel of whale oil, and this successful and cost-effective programme is widely regarded as having had a strong influence on the development of the science of oceanography.

Permanent research stations and programmes

As we have seen, British scientific research in the Antarctic has been almost continuous since 1925, interrupted only by four years of World War II. The present British programme began life as a wartime naval operation, code-named Tabarin, in 1943. Two stations were occupied at the beginning of 1944, with a third in 1945. A further 18 stations have been occupied for varying periods since then. Initially their justification was strategic and political, but scientific programmes were included from the start. For some years priority was given to geographical exploration, mapping and meteorology; later, scientific discovery became more important. After the war, responsibility was transferred to the Colonial Office and the expanded operation was called the Falkland Islands Dependencies Survey (FIDS).

The major British biological research station at Signy Island, South Orkney Islands, where I spent my first two years in the Antarctic.

After the Antarctic Treaty came into force in 1961, the southern portion of the Falklands Islands Dependencies was renamed British Antarctic

Territory, while FIDS became the British Antarctic Survey (BAS). The wide dispersal of the research groups in Britain had disadvantages, so they were brought together in 1976 in a purpose-built research institute in Cambridge (of which I was privileged to be the Director). A large extension to the institute was occupied in 1988. Currently there are five permanent British Antarctic stations, two ships and four aircraft, all in direct contact with the Cambridge headquarters by satellite links.

The United States Antarctic Programme has developed along different lines, and as presently organised is typical of the way a number of other countries have approached the problem. Since 1955 the US programme has been the responsibility of the National Science Foundation (NSF). Naval and Coastguard ships and aircraft provide field support, while the NSF contracts a civilian firm to maintain its stations and to provide support staff. Scientific research is also funded by the NSF, in the form of peer-reviewed grants to university applicants. In addition, some other US government agencies have Antarctic programmes.

Australia's Casey Station, in Greater Antarctica, 60°17'S, 110°32'E.

International co-operation in science

It was in 1875 that the idea of international scientific collaboration at the poles was first proposed, with the aim of collecting data on meteorology, magnetics, auroras and ice. The result was the first Polar Year in 1882-83. A second Polar Year was organised fifty years later in 1932-33, involving 44 nations and scientific bodies. Both of these Polar Years had coincided with years when the sun's activity was at its lowest, but so much interest was aroused by the 1932-33 event that a third Polar Year was proposed for the next solar maximum, just 25 years later.

In 1951 this scientific programme was expanded to cover the globe, and accordingly it was renamed International Geophysical Year (IGY). Antarctica was chosen as an area for particular attention because of its influence on global weather, atmosphere and oceans. Throughout the planning period politics were firmly kept in the background, although elsewhere the 'Cold War' held sway. The USA agreed to establish a key station at the South

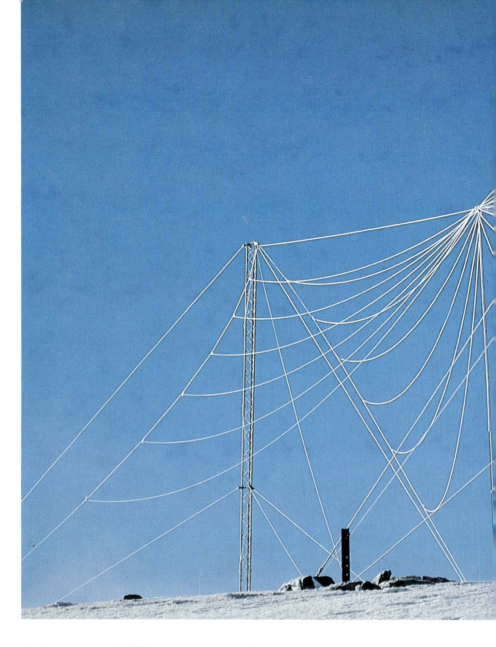

Pole, and the USSR to set up similar research stations at the South Geomagnetic Pole and the Pole of Inaccessibility (the point furthest from all Antarctic coasts).

In 1957 twelve nations began their eighteen-month period of coordinated data collecting. In all, 50 stations were operational during this period, 47 of them year-round, and the Antarctic population rose to more than five thousand. The United States programme was the largest, but the USSR made a major contribution in many disciplines. At the same time Britain established the station (at Halley Bay on the Weddell Sea) which first began monitoring the ozone layer, something that has since come to have such major implications for mankind.

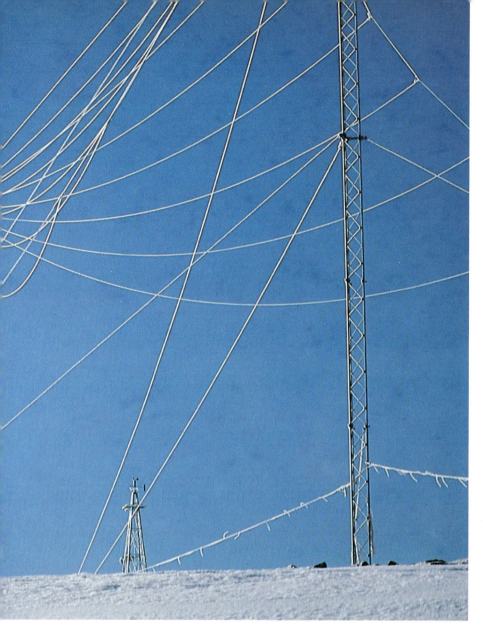

Rime-coated radio aerials.

It was also during this period that the last great Antarctic journey was accomplished: Fuchs' privately-funded Trans Antarctic Expedition, which finally achieved what Shackleton had first set out to do in 1914. Fuchs' team crossed the Antarctic, as planned, in 99 days, and covered 2,180 miles (or roughly 3,500 kilometres). But there were scientific objectives as well: it was this expedition which proved that Greater and Lesser Antarctica were separate entities, and whose measurements allowed the first estimates of the volume of ice in Antarctica. So successful was the International Geophysical Year (despite the Cold War) that it was extended for a further year and the opportunity was taken to set up a permanent system to promote Antarctic science. It also led directly to the signing of the Antarctic Treaty.

The Scientific Committee on Antarctic Research (SCAR)

Inspired by the success of the International Geophysical Year, the Special Committee on Antarctic Research (or SCAR) was established in 1958 by the International Council of Scientific Unions (ISCU), with delegates from each nation actively engaged in Antarctic research, and representatives of relevant unions. In 1961 its name was changed to the Scientific Committee on Antarctic Research.

SCAR is 'charged with the initiation, promotion and coordination of scientific activity in the Antarctic, with a view to framing and reviewing scientific programmes of circumpolar scope and significance.' Within it there are eight permanent Working Groups; and currently eight Groups of Specialists, who examine multidisciplinary problems and provide specialist advice. Since 1959 nearly forty international symposia have been held.

SCAR responds to requests from the Antarctic Treaty Consultative Meetings for advice on Antarctic matters, as well as initiating international research programmes. The most successful of these began in 1976, with a ten-year programme — Biological Investigations of Marine Antarctic Systems and Stocks (BIOMASS) which aimed to gain a deeper understanding of the structure and dynamic functioning of Antarctic marine ecosystems. Such knowledge is essential for future management of the potential living resources of the Antarctic.

In addition to the programmes arranged under the auspices of SCAR, there have been a number of joint studies mounted by individual countries. Examples include the International Antarctic Glaciological Programme, organised by the UK, Australia, France, the USSR and the USA; the Dry Valleys Drilling Project (Japan, New Zealand and the USA); and a study of the Antarctic Circumpolar Current, with the USA, the USSR and Argentina all taking part.

Exploitation and direct human impacts: sealing

Seal stocks were the first natural resource in the Antarctic to be exploited. They were undisturbed by man until after Cook's discovery of South Georgia in 1775, when the sealers extended their depredations southwards across the Polar Front for the first time. At first only Britain and the USA were involved, but they were later joined by Russia, France and other European countries.

Fur seals were the initial focus of interest, because they were more valuable than other species. Discovery was usually followed by indiscriminate killing of both sexes and all ages, which resulted in the near-extinction of local stocks. At this point the sealers simply moved on to the next stock. Decades later another group of sealers might return to 'mop-up' any surviving herds, which (if left alone in the interim) might have begun to increase again. Usually there would be several phases of sealing, each one less profitable than the last.

One of the better documented examples of sealing comes from South Georgia (although even here the records are incomplete). A peak was reached during 1800 to 1801, when 17 British and American vessels took 112,000 fur seal skins. Weddell calculated that by 1822 at least 1.2 million skins had been taken and the population virtually wiped out (it is possible that the original population was of the order of two million or more). After several decades of little or no further depredation, a single vessel took 500 skins in 1870, and five vessels a further 600 in 1875. By the following year, four vessels could only take 110 skins: similar numbers were reportedly taken in 1892 and 1907.

It seems probable that some two to three million, or even more fur seals may have been killed in total, including pups which would not have survived their mothers' deaths. Although this is enormous in terms of individual suffering it was probably relatively insignificant in terms of its impact on the marine ecosystem compared to the effects of whaling or, more recently, Antarctic fishing.

Seal oil also became an important commodity, and one which whalers took (as well as the valuable fur seal skins) right from the beginning of their voyages to the southern seas. Seals were killed as indiscriminately for their oil as they had been for their furs, and the elephant seal oil industry showed a similar pattern of discovery, extermination, recovery and reduced rewards from later voyages. The introduction of petroleum, however, depressed the seal and whale oil markets so far that from the 1870s on sealing was sporadic, with the last visits to South Georgia in 1912.

It is difficult to estimate the total number of southern elephant seals that were killed for their oil during the nineteenth century, but it seems likely to have been at least 750,000, or possibly as much as a million to bring the stocks near to extinction.

By the time of the Seal Fishery Ordinance in 1909 the elephant seal stocks had increased again in numbers, and from then on commercial quotas were set, while fur seals received absolute protection. The coastline of South Georgia was divided into four sealing divisions, three of which were worked in any year (one remaining unworked in rotation). There were also several reserves in which no sealing was permitted. The catch was confined to adult males and to a quota of 2,000 per division, with a closed season from October (later November) to the end of February.

As a result of my research in 1951, I recommended divisional quotas that were based on my stock estimates and instituted other controls. I concluded that the average age of the catch should be 7.5 to 8 years to attain the maximum sustainable yield. The new regulations achieved this, produced an increased daily yield per catcher and increased oil production. But the industry ended in 1964 when whaling at South Georgia ceased due to over-exploitation, dragging the rationally-managed sealing industry with it. This was a very good example — one of the best — of the successful management of an animal resource on scientific principles. In the course of this industry some 260,000 bull elephant seals were taken, with a total biomass of some 500,000 tonnes. Together with the elephant seals killed in the nineteenth century it suggests that the total weight of elephant seals caught was something like a million tonnes, very much greater than the weight of Antarctic fur seals caught but still insignificant compared with the whale catches.

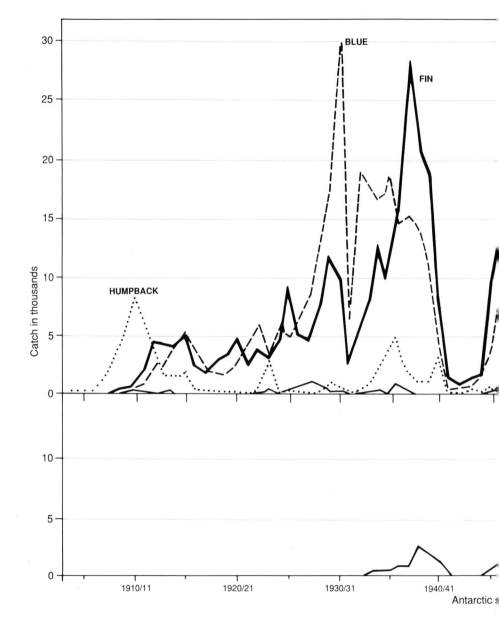

Antarctic whaling

Sperm whales and southern right whales had been hunted on the northern edges of the Southern Ocean from the start of the nineteenth century, but it was not until 1904 that Antarctic whaling really began. C.A. Larsen's whaling station on South Georgia was an immediate success, and by 1914 there were six shore stations, 21 factory ships and 62 catchers operating in the Falklands Islands Dependencies, taking about 10,000 whales a year.

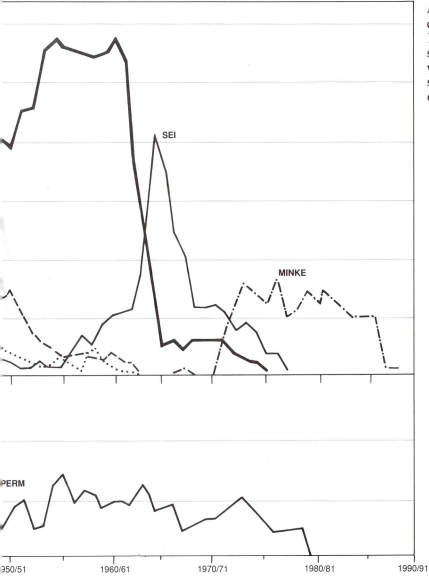

Antarctic whale catches by species, 1904-1989, showing how baleen whale species were successively overhunted.

By the 1929/30 Antarctic season there were over 40 British and Norwegian floating factories and more than 200 whale catcher boats. This led to such an overproduction of whale oil that in 1930/31 the market collapsed, and it was this which forced the industry to set voluntary quotas for the expeditions. These were only partly successful, however, and in 1931 the International Convention for the Regulation of Whaling was drawn up. Henceforth quotas were set in Blue Whale Units (BWU), a measure that lumped all baleen whales together in terms of their oil production, regardless of species. One BWU initially equalled one blue whale, two fin, three humpback, or five sei whales. In 1937 additional international agreements came into force which limited oil production, set minimum lengths for some whales, shortened the hunting season to three months and prohibited the killing of humpbacks on the high seas. In 1938 a sanctuary was created in the Pacific sector where whaling was banned.

In 1946 another International Convention for the Regulation of Whaling was agreed and a permanent Commission and Scientific Committee was set up: these remain the bodies responsible for managing the whale stocks. However, this Convention required that weight be given to the needs of the whaling industry and consumers of whale products, putting the onus of proof on those who wished to reduce the catches. Procedures, also, meant that effectively any of the Commission's decisions had to be unanimous in order to be implemented. And so, until recent years, the economic arguments of the pro-whaling factor (that the industry could not survive without a large catch) carried more weight than the scientific advice that the catches were higher than the various stocks could withstand.

These problems were compounded from an early stage by the BWU system, whose first quota of 16,000 BWUs, set for 1945/46, was then subject only to token changes; so that even by 1962/63 it had only decreased to 15,000 BWUs. The danger of setting quotas in BWUs was that as the larger and more valuable species were depleted the industry could simply switch to smaller species, while still taking some of larger whales. The latter could therefore be driven towards extinction, since normal economic constraints on their hunting did not apply.

It was (and is) extremely difficult to assess the status of whale populations in the ocean. Attempts have been made to estimate their numbers and changes over time, directly from whale sighting cruises, or indirectly using mark-recapture analysis. All methods present problems, which have not yet been resolved. But studies have shown that as whale numbers (and therefore densities) decline the animals breed more frequently, and at younger ages. The natural death rate may also decline. The stocks decline if catches exceed a level sustainable by the population, but if populations are then protected they can increase by between seven and thirteen per cent a year, depending on species.

A critical point was reached in 1960, when the qualitative evidence of whale population decline was becoming unequivocal. The fact that one single member of the Scientific Committee did not accept the evidence, however, enabled the industry to argue that proof was lacking because scientific opinion was not unanimous. A committee of four independent scientists experienced in population dynamics was appointed, and made its final report in 1964. They recommended complete protection for blue and humpback whales, reduction of fin whale catches, the elimination of the BWU system and the setting of separate catch quotas for each species.

The International Whaling Commission responded half-heartedly, reducing the quota for 1963/64 by giving humpback whales complete protection and blue whales partial protection. The turning point came when the Committee of Four's prediction that such a high quota could not be achieved turned out to be correct. Yet it was not until the 1967/68 season that a rational policy was instituted, the quota then being 3,200 BWU's, but the BWU was not abolished until as late as 1972.

In 1972 the United Nations Conference on the Environment approved a resolution calling for a ten-year moratorium on commercial whaling. It was opposed by Japan and the USSR and was not implemented. A decade later, however, the International Whaling Commission approved just such a moratorium. This was intended to be a temporary measure to give time for research to resolve serious disagreements on abundance estimates and sustainable yields, and there is to be a review not later than 1990.

More than 1.3 million whales have been killed by commercial whalers in the Southern Ocean, representing a biomass of around 70 million tonnes, and this has caused a major disturbance to the oceanic marine ecosystem. With species catch limits in place, the numbers of most kinds of Antarctic whales should have increased over the past 15 years, but it is not known whether severely depleted species like the blue whale can recover their former abundance, even with complete protection. What is agreed by whale scientists is that if it does ever happen it will be an extremely slow process, taking decades at least — and perhaps centuries.

Fish and krill harvesting

Commercial interest in Antarctic fish stocks dates back to the beginning of whaling at South Georgia in 1904. Whalers noticed large numbers of fish over the shelf around the island, but for whatever reason this potential fishery was not developed. The first successful exploratory fishing was undertaken by the USSR in the Scotia Sea , and this led to commercial fishing for South Georgia cod around South Georgia in the late 1960s. From a few hundred tonnes in 1967/68 the catches at South Georgia rapidly increased to 90,000 tonnes in 1968/69 and peaked at 400,000 tonnes the following season, after which they declined dramatically.

In 1978/79 the fishery extended to the South Shetlands and Joinville Island, and the catches (mainly of icefish) again peaked early and then declined.

The Antarctic fishery followed the pattern of other fisheries and the whaling industry, beginning with rapid overfishing of preferred species, followed by the discovery of new stocks, new species to exploit and new fishing grounds. Antarctic fish, because of their relatively late maturity and slow growth rates, appear to be especially vulnerable to overfishing. In the two decades since the 1960s some 5.5 million tonnes of fish have been caught. This is small by world standards, and in comparison to the catches of the whales, but the local impact of overfishing may be significant (for example by removing one source of food during the breeding period of South Georgia's seabirds).

Russian mother ship and stern trawler near South Georgia.

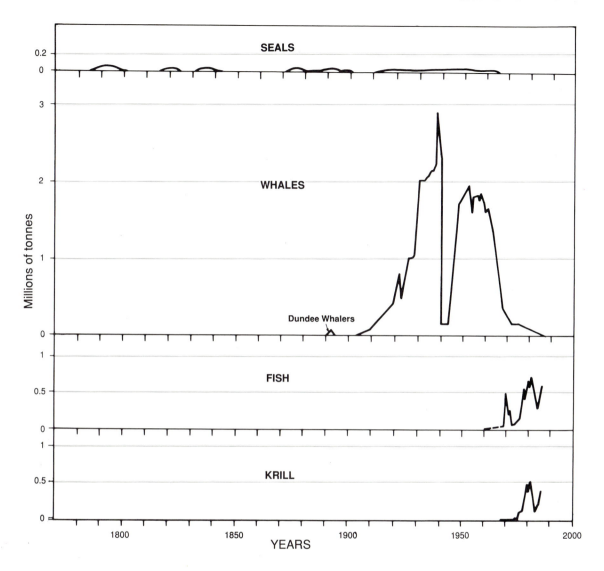

The krill fishery began much later, and its expansion seems to have taken the place, to some extent, of the reduced fish catches. Unlike fin fish, krill has to be processed within a few hours of catching, and after several other unsuccessful attempts, a method was developed using a large midwater trawl with a fine mesh and a mouth 200 square metres wide. Swarms were detected using an echo-sounder and catching rates of ten to twenty tonnes per hour, 100 tonnes a day were achieved — more than the factory could handle continuously. Despite the discovery of a solution to these processing problems, inital Soviet production of krill paste and cheese for human consumption was not a commerical success. Most of the subsequent krill catch has ended up as a food supplement for domestic animals, although it contains hazardously high levels of flouride and it has proved to be more expensive than fishmeal.

Human impacts: the tonnages of commercial catches of seals, whales, fish and krill, 1784-1988.

181

Altogether some three million tonnes of krill have been harvested since the 1960s, but this is a very small figure compared with an undoubted potential of tens of millions of tonnes a year, if a market for krill could be developed. Nevertheless, if the marketing problems are overcome, the impact of krill harvesting on the oceanic ecosystems could be enormous, especially if fishing is concentrated in one area, for example in the Scotia Sea. Here sustained local catches could have very adverse effects on other krill consumers such as seabird and fur seal colonies. Chile, East Germany, Japan, South Korea, Poland and the USSR have all been involved in krill fishing, but so far only Japan and the USSR have made significant commercial catches.

The Japanese market a variety of krill products.

The impact of mammals introduced by man

Reindeer in front of Neumayer Glacier and the Allardyce Range on South Georgia.

Wherever man has gone he has introduced alien species, often with damaging consequences for the natural environment, and the sub-Antarctic (though not the continent itself) is no exception. The plant communities of the Sub-Antarctic are particularly sensitive to grazing, since they evolved in the absence of grazing animals. The success of ground-nesting birds, too, has only been possible thanks to a lack of terrestrial predators.

Various domestic grazing animals have been introduced in the past, including cattle, goats, sheep, moufflon, horses and pigs. Most of these have not become permanently established, but rats, mice, rabbits, reindeer and cats have. Shipwrecks deposited the first rats, probably around the end of the nineteenth century. Not all islands support rat populations, however, even where sealers have been active in the past. Oddly, while all the other islands have the black rat species associated with ships, South Georgia's rats are brown. These rats have exterminated the indigenous South Georgia pipit on the main island.

183

Mice have had no impact on the birds and probably little effect on vegetation, but the rabbits which were introduced to Kerguelen and Macquarie Islands during the 1870s have all but destroyed the Kerguelen cabbage in the areas they have colonised. Unsuccessful attempts have been made to control the rabbits including the introduction of the myxoma virus.

The introduction of reindeer at South Georgia and Kerguelen has also done substantial damage to the natural environment. The situation at South Georgia is best documented. Three groups of reindeer were introduced there between 1911 and 1925 by whalers, but only the first and last established themselves on a permanent basis. By the mid 1950s the first group had increased its numbers to several thousand, while the third group's population grew more slowly, peaking at 800 in 1973 and later falling to around 450. Tussock grass in the reindeer ranges has been badly overgrazed in places, but the main effect has been on the macrolichens, which are scarce or absent in the grazed areas and are susceptible to trampling, as are the mosses.

Domestic cats were introduced to Macquarie Island before 1820, and now number about 250-500, taking some 57,000 rabbits, 46,000 prions and 11,000 white-headed petrels every year; they have also exterminated two endemic birds, the banded rail and a parakeet. At Kerguelen an early population had died out by 1874 but cats were then reintroduced in the 1950s. By 1973 there were two to three thousand, killing an estimated 1.2 million birds (particularly blue petrels and prions) annually. On Marion Island two cats were introduced in 1949: by 1979 their two thousand descendants had become major predators, hunting mainly burrowing petrels, as well as mice and the occasional penguin. They are estimated to take 455,000 birds every year, and they have exterminated the island's diving petrels.

Almost all of these introductions have had adverse, and in some cases catastrophic results, sometimes leading to the extinction of an indigenous plant or animal species. They are one of the more unpleasant legacies of man's arrival in Antarctica.

The potential environmental impacts of mineral exploration and exploitation

As we have already seen, the Antarctic is quite unlike the Arctic, which is an ocean basin surrounded by developed nations with indigenous populations and modern settlements. There are no indigenous populations in Antarctica, and so no pressure for development. The continent is surrounded by a wide, deep, and exceptionally stormy ocean, thick with hazardous pack-ice and icebergs.

Despite plenty of mineral 'occurrences', very few deposits have been identified and 98 per cent of the bedrock is hidden by ice. The only known 'hardrock' mineral deposits are low-grade iron in the Prince Charles Mountains and low-grade coal in the Transantarctic Mountains, both in Greater Antarctica. The prime target for exploration is the Dufek Massif, which has been compared with the Bushveld Complex in South Africa, source of 85 per cent of the world's platinum. But the Dufek Massif is smaller than the Bushveld, largely covered by the ice sheet, and 550 kilometres from the nearest sea, which is fringed by floating ice shelves and infested with very dense pack-ice and large icebergs. There is also no certainty that significant mineral deposits will be found.

Again, there is little evidence of major oil or gas reserves, whether or not they would prove economically exploitable. Only the first of four geological conditions associated with exploitable petroleum reserves is known to be met in the Antarctic. The costs of exploration, let alone development, would be enormous even by Arctic standards, where hundreds of billions of dollars have been spent in the Canadian Arctic Islands, without as yet any commercial production there of oil or gas. Also new technology would have to be developed to cope with the unique problems posed by Antarctic conditions — particularly the thick ice-cover on land, and the great depths of water, dense pack-ice and vast icebergs at sea, which threaten not only ships and drilling rigs, but also sea floor installations at depths down to 250 metres. The costs of developing such new technology are unknown, as are the future economic returns in terms of metallic mineral and oil prices. In any case higher prices would lead first to extraction from currently uneconomic reserves in more favourable locations.

Copper mineralization is indicated here by the bright green patches of malachite, seen in many localities in the Antarctic Peninsula.

Let us suppose that, despite these incalculable difficulties, exploration and exploitation of Antarctic mineral and hydrocarbon resources began. What would be the likely environmental consequences?

Oil spills are potential threats to exploitable living marine resources in general and krill in particular, and also to penguin colonies. Oil and gas extraction would involve drilling, pumping, storage and transportation, with all their attendant risks. Blowouts, whether on land or at sea, would take longer to get under control in such a harsh environment. Oil spills, from rigs or tankers (which would be extremely vulnerable to icebergs) could be trapped under shelf or sea ice, or incorporated into it. Unfortunately — in this context — there have been no major Arctic oil spills, so there is no relevant experience to call upon. However, oil spills would be localised in their effect within the vastness of the Antarctic, and even a major blowout might be expected to affect little more than 80-100 square kilometres of the 36 million square kilometres of ocean south of the Polar Front. Similarly coastal construction, although likely to have significant local effects, can be compared to the effects of naturally occurring iceberg ploughing.

Sedimentary basins lie beneath the ice sheet in Greater and Lesser Antarctica, also on the continental margin and under the ocean floor at depths greater than 2000 metres. They may contain hydrocarbons.

Even severe local impacts, such as those already pointed out, are probably not likely to be significant overall because of the large area of the Antarctic. The greatest concern is over persistent large-scale effects even if the level of contamination is relatively low. Airborne pollutants, for example, could have very extensive effects, even though most human activities would be concentrated on the two per cent of ice free land and be minimised by winds carrying dust particles out to sea. Dust, sulphur dioxide and aerosols all reduce the value of the Antarctic ice sheet for monitoring global pollution and climatic change.

Overall it seems that the most serious potential impact is likely to be due to dust darkening the surface of the ice: this could lower its reflectivity, with global consequences for the world's climate. It could also promote surface melting of the ice cap.

Indirect human impacts: the record in the ice

The oldest ice in the Antarctic ice cap was formed from snow that probably fell half a million years ago: ice older than that has flowed out to sea, where it has been lost as icebergs or by melting from below the ice shelves. As snow crystals form they incorporate, or 'scavenge', constituents of the atmosphere like rock dust, volcanic ash and sea salts, as well as industrial products like insecticide and heavy metal wastes. As it settles it also traps atmospheric gases like oxygen, carbon dioxide and methane.

When the snow increases in density and turns to ice all these constituents are trapped, forming a permanent record of conditions at the time the various layers were formed. Engineers have developed efficient equipment to collect long ice cores, and over the last 15 years analytical methods have been developed to detect and measure the inclusions in different strata of these cores.

Because the impurities are at extremely low levels the methods used must be very sensitive; the Antarctic ice sheet is the cleanest natural area in the world. Different levels in a core can be dated by counting the annual layers, like tree rings or in other ways. Where layers of volcanic ash, or in recent years radioactivity occur they may be correlated with a known volcanic eruption or with a nuclear test explosion.

Antarctica's remoteness from human population centres and industry means that the archive in the ice can be used as a standard for comparison, and the pre-industrial levels in the ice cores provide a natural baseline against which increases in the global level of pollutants, due to human activities, can be measured.

They show us that in the last 200 years there has been a 25 per cent increase in the amount of carbon dioxide (CO_2) in the atmosphere. Methane levels have doubled since 1650. Toxic heavy metals have also increased in the last two centuries, although concentrations are still quite low.

The 'greenhouse effect'

Incoming radiation from the sun warms up the ground, which in its turn generates long-wave infra-red radiation. Some clouds and gases (notably water vapour and carbon dioxide) absorb infra-red radiation, a process that causes them to heat up. This heat is then distributed unevenly by currents throughout the atmosphere, which alters the balance between incoming and outgoing radiation. As a result, the temperature of the whole atmosphere will rise (particularly near to the ground).

This so-called 'greenhouse effect' has been known since the last century, but it is only since 1975 that it has been recognized as a really serious problem for mankind: possibly the most serious one that we face.

Atmospheric carbon dioxide produced by human activities still makes the largest contribution to this effect, and the analysis of bubbles in the Antarctic ice cores indicates that concentrations, as we have just seen, have increased by about 25 per cent since 1850. The annual rate of increase is now about three per cent a year.

King penguins examining a solar panel at the camp in St. Andrews Bay, South Georgia, where Cindy Buxton, Annie Price and three BAS men sat out the Argentine invasion, in 1982, the first and one hopes the last armed conflict in the Antarctic.

It is the burning of the world's forests and the use of fossil fuels which has released all this carbon dioxide, which was previously locked up in organic compounds. However, the rate of increase would be greater but for the oceans (of which the Southern Ocean is thought to be the most important), which absorb half the carbon dioxide produced and whose biological and physical processes gradually pump the carbon towards the bottom; the turnover rate, however, ranges from 100 to 1,500 years.

Despite this, the effects of atmospheric carbon dioxide continue to increase. A doubling of the 1850 figure would alone mean a rise in global air temperature of 2°C.

Although CO_2 is the most abundant greenhouse gas, it is known that other greenhouse gases are also increasing for similar reasons. These other gases include methane (which now has an effect equivalent to 36 per cent of that due to carbon dioxide), ozone, nitrous oxide and the man-made chlorofluorocarbons (CFCs). The combined warming from these other gases is already three per cent more than the effect caused by all the carbon dioxide, and it is still increasing.

The level of methane is increasing at 1.2 percent a year. It is produced by cattle and other grazing animals, by decomposition of vegetable matter for instance in paddy fields, by coal mining and the burning of fossil fuels.

Unlike methane, the CFCs (which are also implicated in the destruction of the ozone layer) are entirely man-made. Their production — for use in spray cans, refrigerants and foam-blowing — has increased rapidly to nearly a million tonnes a year, and the two most important have estimated lifespans of 75 and 110 years before they are broken down. They are very efficient greenhouse gases and one molecule of CFC has the same greenhouse warming effect as 10,000 molecules of carbon dioxide.

Nitrous oxide is also increasing at 0.3 per cent a year, the result of microbial action in the soil and the breakdown of nitrate fertilisers; it has a lifespan of 170 years in the atmosphere. With the increased use of nitrate fertilisers even underground watercourses, or aquifers, are now releasing nitrous oxide into the atmosphere.

Within the next twenty years the combined effect of the greenhouse gases could take global warming higher than at any time in the last 100,000 years. Even a three per cent global warming would mean a warmer overall climate than at any time in the past two to three million years; and this degree of warming will be greater nearer the poles, perhaps by 7°C. But the most recent models have suggested global rises of up to five per cent, and temperatures up by 12°C in the polar regions.

Recent analyses show that in global terms 1987 was the warmest year since records began, with 1981 and 1983 the next warmest. The rise is greatest in the southern hemisphere, where seven of the eight warmest years occurred during the 1980s. The warming phase seems to be well under way.

This warming will have widespread effects, varying from region to region. Cold seasons will become shorter and warmer seasons longer, so that the annual range of temperatures will be reduced. Higher evaporation will lead to drier soils, but a wetter atmosphere, with rainfall up 7-11 per cent overall, though reduced in some regions. The droughts in recent years in the sub-Saharan Sahel region may well be among the first signs that the greenhouse effect is gathering pace.

The Antarctic has a crucial significance in this context, mainly because of the direct effect of higher air temperatures on the ice cap and the ice shelves, and indirectly through effects on global sea levels. If the ice sheet melted completely — probably a remote possibility — there would be a 60-metre rise in world sea levels, but a rise of one metre is likely within a century.

This sounds like a small change, but even such a relatively minor increase would have serious consequences for low-lying countries. In Bangladesh it would, for instance, affect 12 per cent of the land, nine per cent of the human population and eliminate 11 per cent of all agricultural production. The Andaman Islands, off Burma in the Bay of Bengal, would disappear completely. Like all other sea-level cities and ports, London and New York would have major problems.

Nothing is certain, however, for a global increase in evaporation rates due to warming might lead to increased Antarctic precipitation, expanding the volume of ice and possibly lowering the sea level. And the various postulated effects could cancel one another out to varying degrees. Whatever happens, the rate of change will be crucial; mankind may be able to react to major changes which happen over centuries, but we stand little chance of success if the timescale is nearer 20-50 years.

The ice sheet not only records, but also responds to (and causes) changes in climate and sea level. So it is important to monitor any changes in the total volume of Antarctic ice. The ice sheet of Lesser Antarctica is most vulnerable because much of it is grounded below sea level at relatively shallow depths. A rise in global sea level due solely to the expansion of the oceans by warming could cause these grounded ice shelves to float, break up, drift into lower latitudes and melt. Although earlier very pessimistic estimates have since been discounted, there are signs that this process may already have begun. It is estimated that the complete melting of even this comparatively small and thin ice sheet would alone produce a sea level rise of five metres.

Research and monitoring in the Antarctic can give early warning of such global changes. One method looks at the zones where ice shelves begin to float, gradually separating from their rock beds. Such zones are known as grounding lines and react sensitively to alterations in climate, as well as to local changes in the flow of the ice sheet. Grounding lines have been mapped using sensitive tilt meters, which measure where tidal flexing of the ice surface begins. Anomalies in the position of grounding lines could provide the first unequivocal indication that the ice sheet is about to break up. The extent of the Antarctic pack ice is another good indicator of climatic change, and satellite measurements of its area will continue to be important.

The destruction of the ozone layer over the Antarctic

Something else which is happening in Antarctica has serious implications for mankind. Popularly known as the 'ozone hole', it is really a drastic thinning of the ozone layer above four per cent of the earth's surface in spring. This is perhaps the best example to date of the importance of Antarctic research, for without it we would still be in blissful ignorance of a massive global problem which has extremely serious implications for all kinds of living organisms on earth.

Life on earth depends on ozone as much as on oxygen or water, because the ozone layer filters out lethal ultra-violet radiation. Paradoxically, ozone is itself a toxic gas which is poisonous to plants and animals even in small quantities. The ozone layer exists because oxygen (produced by living

A map, based on satellite data shows ozone levels in the atmosphere over the Southern Hemisphere on 15 October 1987. The ozone 'hole' (black, pink, purple) is centred on Antarctica.

organisms on the ground) enters the atmosphere where it is continuously changed into ozone by the action of sunlight. Ozone is also produced by electrical discharges in the atmosphere, and at ground level by the action of sunlight on car exhaust gases and industrial emissions.

The processes are reversible, so ozone is continually being produced and continually destroyed, with a turnover rate of about 18 months. During this time it tends to drift from the equator towards the poles, where the layer is at its thickest. The extremely tenuous ozone layer is found at altitudes of 12-25 kilometres above the Earth's surface; it is present in very low concentrations, such that if it were all concentrated at the atmospheric pressure at sea level it would form a layer only about three millimetres thick.

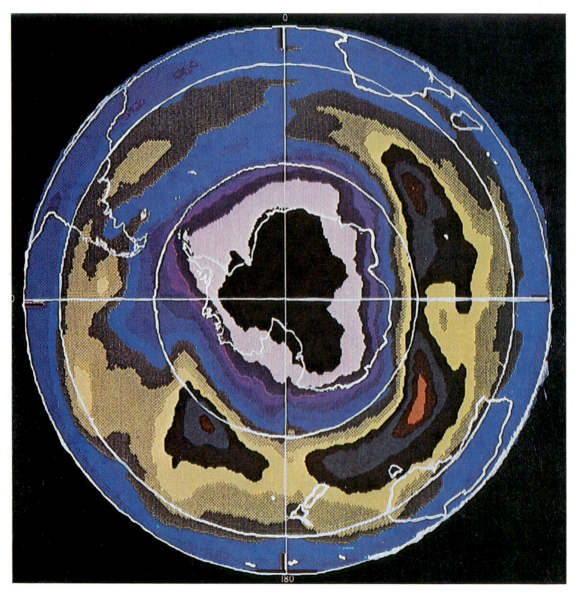

The October average ozone levels observed overhead the British Antarctic Survey Halley Station, 76°S.

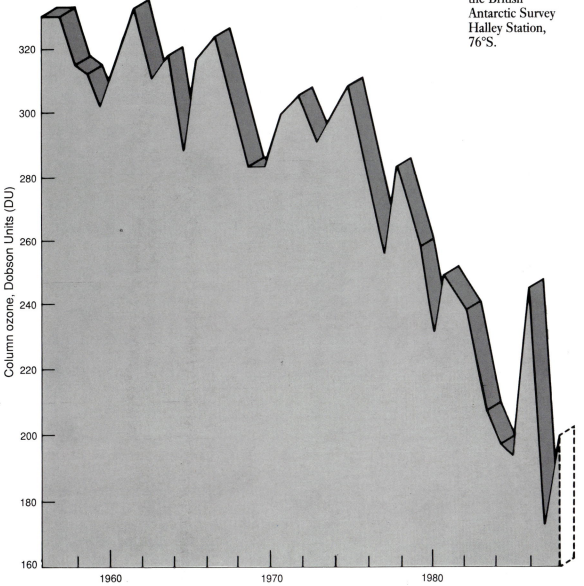

In 1982, as a result of observations by British Antarctic Survey (BAS) scientists at Halley Station on the eastern shore of the Weddell Sea, depletion of the ozone over the Antarctic was suspected. Observations had been made there since 1957, and eventually it became apparent that the amount of ozone present each spring (when the sun warms the atmosphere after the long polar night) had declined from springtime levels in previous years.

By 1984 BAS was sure that there had been a decline and the results were announced. It was also shown that the ozone depletion at Halley corresponded to increases in the amounts of the CFCs which were being measured there. A re-examination of previously-rejected US satellite data confirmed the BAS finding that a dramatic spring thinning of the ozone layer was occurring, and, in addition, that a large 'hole', covering the entire continent, was developing each spring.

This trend has continued, and the 1987 'ozone hole' was the largest ever, with more than half the total ozone being destroyed over 30-40 days that spring. The damage was reversed in the summer of 1988, but did not recover to the 1970s levels.

In August 1986 balloon flights into the ozone hole over Antarctica showed that there was depletion at altitudes between 12 and 20 kilometres. This confirmed that the ozone loss must be due to a catalytic sequence. A massive Airborne Antarctic Ozone Experiment was mounted from August 1987, in which NASA took the lead. Two aircraft repeatedly sampled conditions in the ozone hole at altitudes of 12 and 20 kilometres. Measurements of ozone, aerosols, water and various chemicals established beyond doubt the role of CFCs in damaging the ozone layer over Antarctica.

CFCs, first developed in 1930, are very important commercially; they are chemically stable, non-toxic and non-inflammable. They are used as solvents, for cleaning semi-conductor components in the electronics industry, for blowing plastic foams and as refrigerants. But predominantly they are used as propellants in aerosol spray cans.

The most commonly used CFCs are F-11 and F-12 which survive in the atmosphere before breaking down over about 75 and 110 years respectively. Production of these two CFCs alone reached 800,000 tons a year by the early 1970s and has only fallen slightly since. Total CFC production exceeds a million tons a year. Even if their release into the atmosphere were to be totally stopped now they would still be actively destroying the ozone layer at the end of the next century.

The reason ozone loss is so pronounced over the Antarctic continent is due to its unique atmospheric systems. During the long night of the Antarctic winter the steep temperature gradient that develops between high and low latitudes on the earth tends to lead to a belt of westerly winds reaching high altitudes — the polar vortex — which is stable and intense, effectively sealing off the atmosphere over Antarctica from lower latitudes, and making the air above Antarctica very cold and still. In 1987 the ozone hole was actually smaller than the polar vortex, its border closer to the outline of the Antarctic continent.

Extreme cold within the polar vortex leads to the formation of Polar Stratospheric Clouds (PSCs) at high altitudes. Their presence over the poles has long been known, but it is now thought that they have a pivotal effect in removing ozone. The polar flights in the spring of 1987 showed that the PSCs were stretched right across the polar vortex where very low temperatures prevailed (down to -90°C at 20 kilometres). Inside the vortex CFCs were at very low levels, but the chlorine monoxide they produce when they break down was at several hundred times greater concentrations there than at the same heights in mid-latitudes. The flights showed that the boundary of the ozone hole was sharply defined, and there was a very close inverse correlation between ozone and chlorine monoxide: curves showing quantities of the two mirrored each other almost exactly, with ozone falling where chlorine monoxide concentrations rose.

The chemical reactions which cause this effect are still imperfectly understood (they are processes which are known to occur naturally nowhere else on earth), but the chlorine cycle is probably the most significant of them. A single chlorine atom is thought to be able to knock out possibly as many as 10,000 molecules of ozone.

The 1988 ozone hole was very much less pronounced than in 1987, and less than in 1985 and 1986. It has recently been predicted that the 1989 ozone hole will again be much greater, because there may be a quasi-biennial oscillation, owing to year to year changes in the dynamical activity of the atmosphere.

The hole may not fill in summer, but parts of it drift bodily away from Antarctica as transient mini-holes or eddies, to mix with air in lower latitudes. It has been suggested that in odd-numbered years when the hole is very well developed the lack of ozone in the stratosphere absorbing solar energy means that conditions remain very cold and stable, maintaining the hole and holding back the incoming chlorine-rich air, thus reducing the ozone-reduction rate. Conversely, in even-numbered years when the hole is less well established, ozone remains present to absorb radiation, warming the atmosphere and allowing more chlorine to enter — to cause a more pronounced hole the following spring. If the biennial oscillation is confirmed by future data this could be a possible mechanism, but the situation remains very complex and uncertain.

The reduction is not only confined to the Antarctic polar vortex in spring; there are other changes at other seasons and in other regions including the Arctic. Ozone-deficient air from Antarctica has a diluting effect on the southern hemisphere as a whole, where ozone appears to have decreased by five per cent or more at all latitudes south of 60°S. And in the northern hemisphere (between latitudes 53° and 64°N), despite less extreme conditions, there was a six per cent decline in winter ozone concentrations between 1969 and 1986. Early in 1989 results from research flights over the Arctic showed that the ozone layer there is 'primed for destruction', with very large quantities of chlorine monoxide present. The Arctic ozone hole is less obvious than in the Antarctic but is more threatening to populated parts of the world. Over the whole of our planet the ozone layer has declined so far by perhaps 1-2 per cent overall.

Research continues on the causes: but what can mankind expect as a result? First comes the likely direct effects of increased ultra-violet radiation on life on earth, including people; then there is the effect on world climates due to the alteration of the global heat balance.

Ozone is the only substance in the atmosphere which absorbs UVB, the biologically active radiation band from the sun, to which all life is particularly sensitive. Experiments have shown that UVB kills phytoplankton near the surface of the sea, and almost certainly has effects on invertebrates such as krill. UVB also damages most crops and reduces yields. UVB does its damage by attacking substances such as DNA, the carrier of genetic information, altering its message and even causing death. This can cause localised skin cancers in animals, including humans, or more serious untreatable general skin cancer or melanoma.

It has been calculated that for each one per cent reduction in the concentration of ozone in the stratosphere there is a two per cent increase in UV radiation, a five per cent increase in the number of non-malignant skin cancers and a one per cent increase in mortality from malignant melanoma.

But skin cancer is only one of the known risks from increased exposure to UV radiation. Like the acquired immune deficiency syndrome (AIDS) it also affects the human immune system, and it causes cataracts (because the eye lens is a strong absorber of these wavelengths).

The second class of effects of depletion of the ozone layer, those on climate, contributing to the greenhouse effect by allowing warming of the atmosphere near the ground, are also alarming. In the southern hemisphere spring of 1987 the loss was not evenly distributed and at certain altitudes 97 per cent of the ozone was found to have vanished.

The CFCs which are destroying the ozone layer are, then, potentially disastrous for mankind, and an immediate major reduction in their production — by 95 per cent or more — is called for; the gradual 50 percent reduction agreed by the international Montreal Protocol in 1987 is clearly too little. CFCs are very persistent: they do not interact with living organisms, dissolve in the oceans, or wash out in rain.

What seems very clear is that the chemical interactions involved are extremely complex, and the net result of all these processes completely unpredictable. The safest strategy, therefore, is to take action to minimise human impacts on the atmosphere.

Antarctic politics: the Antarctic Treaty

During the late 1940s the United States became concerned about the development of political conflicts in the Antarctic, particularly the East-West Cold War and the Antarctic Peninsula dispute between Britain, Argentina and Chile. In 1948 it proposed that Antarctica be ruled by an eight-power condominium or by United Nations trusteeship. This idea was not taken up and it was another ten years before there was progress.

The US government finally took the initiative in May 1958 by proposing to the eleven other nations active in Antarctica that a treaty should be drawn

up to set aside the continent for scientific use only. After 60 secret meetings a conference was set up in Washington in October 1959, and the Treaty was signed on 1 December of that year. After ratification by the twelve original signatory states it entered into force on 23 June 1961.

The Treaty covers all land and ice shelves south of 60°S latitude, but high seas remain subject to international law. It stipulates that Antarctica should forever 'be used exclusively for peaceful purposes' and 'not become the scene or object of international discord'. Nuclear explosions and disposal of radioactive wastes are prohibited as 'measures of a military nature', territorial claims are frozen for its duration. There are provisions for exchange of information and personnel and for inspection of stations, installations and equipment by treaty-state observers.

There are now twenty states with consultative status under the Treaty and a further eighteen that have acceded. These governments represent 80 per cent of the world's population, developed and developing countries, east and west, north and south, giving the lie to allegations that it is an exclusive club.

The logo of the international programme of Biological Investigations of Marine Antarctic Systems and Stocks (BIOMASS) includes a blue whale and a krill.

197

Weddell seal
mother and her
pup, protected by
the Convention for
the Conservation of
Antarctic Seals
(1972).

The development of the Antarctic Treaty System

Conservation measures have been an important concern of the Treaty
states, starting in 1964 with the Agreed Measures for the Conservation of
Antarctic Flora and Fauna. The Agreed Measures are generally working
well and statistics have been exchanged and published. However, France's
recent decision to build an aircraft runway in Adelie Land stimulated
protests because of the alleged effects of construction and subsequent
operations on seabird colonies.

These and other arrangements under the Antarctic Treaty could not give
protection to seals in the sea or on floating ice, because states expressly
reserved their rights to the high seas. So a separate agreement was needed
and in 1972 a Convention for the Conservation of Antarctic Seals (CCAS)

was concluded. This came into force in 1978. The Convention applies to the seas south of 60°S, with provision for reporting of catches made in the pack ice even to the north of this latitude. An Annex specifies measures for conservation, scientific study and rational and humane use of seal resources; these measures may be amended. Permissible annual catches are specified in the Annex, deliberately set at low levels. This convention has been very successful and is a good example of a conservation agreement concluded before problems have developed.

The most important current problems are overfishing of Antarctic fish, the expanding catch of krill and the potential development of a squid fishery. Any significant catch of krill would affect the populations of krill predators, and it is no longer sufficient to consider krill and its consumers as a series of separate species, ignoring the interactions between them.

Following the example of CCAS, a Convention for the Conservation of Antarctic Marine Living Resources (CCAMLR) was concluded in 1980 and came into force in 1982. Its objective is the conservation (including rational use) of all Antarctic marine life and it applies to waters south of the Antarctic Convergence (the Antarctic Polar Front). Harvesting is to be applied in accordance with stated conservation principles; no harvested population is to be allowed to decrease below those levels which ensure its stable continuation; ecological relationships between harvested, dependent and related populations are to be maintained, and depleted populations restored; and changes are to be prevented that cannot be reversed within a few decades.

Like the other measures under the Treaty system, this convention is unusual in addressing conservation needs in advance of actual commercial activities, except in the case of demersal (bottom-living) fish around South Georgia, where industry had already depleted the stocks.

Finally there is the knotty problem of mineral resources. The Antarctic Treaty makes no reference to minerals because at the time it was drawn up it was recognised that agreement would have been impossible. Another reason is that Antarctica's potential mineral resources remain unknown, though speculative estimates have been made. It was, however, clear that negotiations would be more likely to succeed if they were carried out before a serious commercial interest had developed. Formal talks between governments began in 1982 in Wellington, New Zealand, where the final meeting also took place in June 1988. The resulting Convention on the Regulation of Antarctic Mineral Resource Activities (or CRAMRA) was adopted on 2 June 1988. It remains to be signed and ratified before it enters into force.

CRAMRA applies to the area south of 60°S, and includes the seabed up to the deep seas beyond the continental shelf. The basic idea is to agree to obligations and machinery necessary to establish a legal basis for determining where and under what conditions mineral resources exploration and development should occur. In summary, the initial stage of prospecting would not require prior authorisation, but would be subject to general environmental and safety standards. The next stages, exploration and development, require authorisations to grant exclusive rights to individual operators. Then specific requests for exploration and development would be elaborated and specific proposals would be considered. For each area a Regulatory Commission under CRAMRA would then be responsible for judging the specific application, and if approval were given, monitor the conduct of any operations, including the review of proposals to proceed from the exploration phase to development.

This, then, is the Antarctic Treaty System, which now applies to a tenth of the world's surface. In addition to the three conventions, 164 recommendations have been accepted at the biennial consultative meetings. These recommendations cover matters such as safety, environmental protection, regulation of tourism and exchange of information.

The future arrangements

From 1991 the Antarctic Treaty, which is of unlimited duration and is open for signature by all states, may be reviewed at the request of any one Consultative Party. Despite its undoubted achievements the Treaty has come under attack in recent years from some non-signatory governments and from non-governmental environmental organisations.

The Treaty was conceived as a means of preventing conflict and avoiding super-power controversy over ten per cent of the Earth's surface. The avoidance of conflict remains the primary purpose and science had become almost secondary until very recently, when the crucial importance of Antarctic research for early-warning and monitoring of global problems like the ozone hole suddenly came to the fore.

A small iceberg, sculptured by waves as it repeatedly tilted when pieces broke off.

Shared experience in the Antarctic remains the basis for membership of the Antarctic Treaty System, but the consequences of increased membership could carry the seeds of destruction. New scientific procedures, such as remote-sensing and advanced computing, mean that countries without ground-bases in Antarctica (and therefore currently ineligible voting membership) can make significant contributions, and will expect to have a voice in decision-making. There may be a case for reviewing the qualifications for membership and for helping poorer but genuinely interested newcomers to join. It has also been argued that greater 'transparency' is needed in the

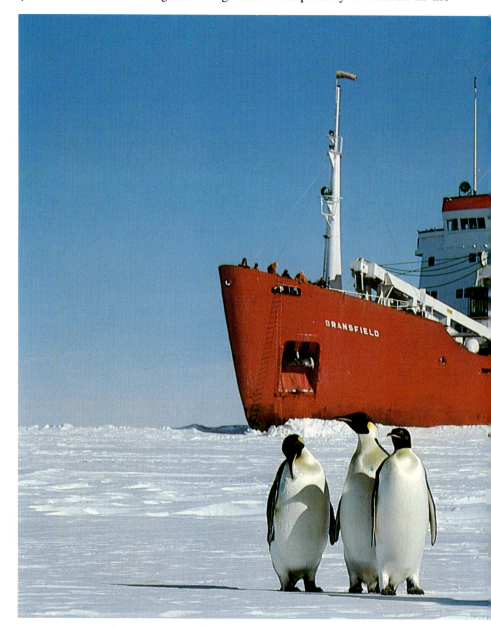

workings of the System, as is an improved flow of information both within it and to the outside world. All this points to the need for a permanent secretariat to improve internal coordination.

It is uncertain whether the question of sovereignty is receding. Certainly, in successive Antarctic Treaty System agreements sovereignty has become less relevant, but nationalism is increasing around the world. It seems unlikely, therefore, that differences over sovereignty will be easily resolved, but perhaps they can be kept in check to ensure that the Antarctic will continue to be used for peaceful purposes. Jurisdictional issues can be

The BAS ship RRS Bransfield alongside fast ice near Halley Station.

expected to become crucial, and could raise serious difficulties because of the increasing number of people in the Antarctic, including many visitors brought by the rapidly developing tourist industry, and private individuals not under direct government control.

In short it has been said that the Antarctic Treaty System has been built out of agreement on 'soft' issues and has still to show that it can cope with 'hard' issues, such as jurisdiction and the expected pressures if mineral exploitation becomes a reality. But the consultative parties have shown great ingenuity in adapting the System to meet new requirements; its strength and viability was very clearly demonstrated during the armed conflict in 1982, which did not spread to the Antarctic.

In the long run the need to maintain the Antarctic for peaceful purposes is likely to continue to take precedence over resource utilisation. This policy is now of greater value and importance than even its far-sighted originators could have realised at its inception. Recognition of the impact of man on the physical and biological environment has been highlighted by the discovery of the ozone hole. The appreciation of the importance of the Antarctic in providing early warning of such global disasters gives Antarctic science a new perspective and crucial role.

Signy Island during the winter locked in consolidated pack ice across which drift snow blows.

FURTHER READING

Bonner, W.N. and Walton, D.W.H. (eds), Key Environments – Antarctica. Pergammon Press 1985.

Deacon, G.E.R., The Antarctic Circumpolar Ocean. Cambridge University Press 1984.

Fifield, R., International Research in the Antarctic. Oxford University Press 1987.

Hardy, A., Great Waters. Collins 1967.

King, H.G.R., The Antarctic. Blandford Press 1969.

Laws, R.M. (ed), Antarctic Ecology. (Two volumes). Academic Press 1984.

Lovering, J.F. and Prescott, J.R.V., Last of Lands – Antarctica. Melbourne University Press 1979.

Parsons, A., Antarctica: the next decade. Cambridge University Press 1987.

Triggs, G. (ed), The Antarctic Treaty Regime: Law, Environment and Resources. Cambridge University Press 1987.

Walton, D.W.H. (ed), Antarctic Science. Cambridge University Press 1987.

Index

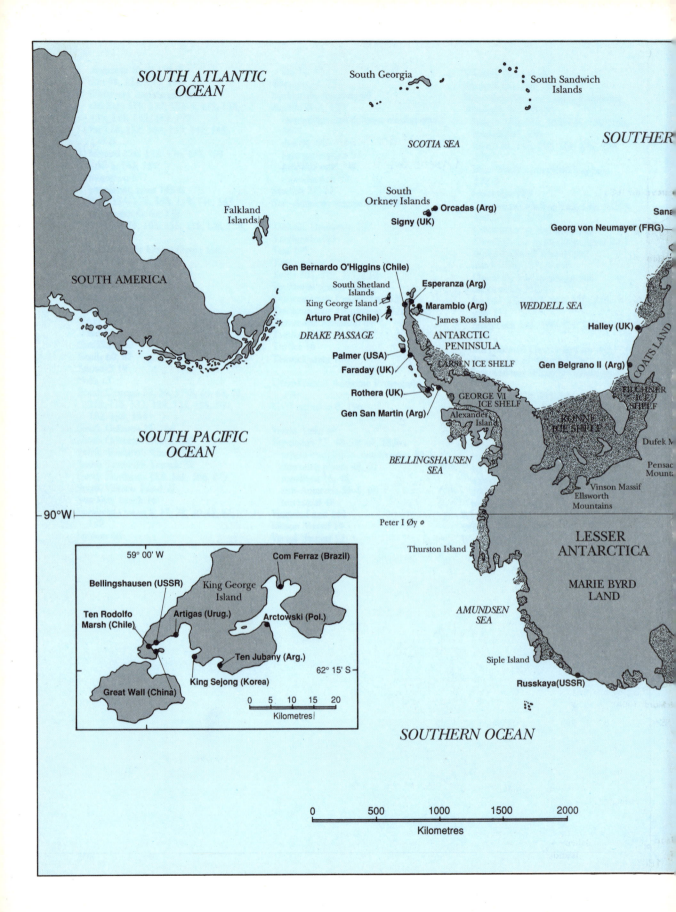

SOUTH ATLANTIC
OCEAN

South Georgia

South Sandwich
Islands

SCOTIA SEA

SOUTHER

South
Orkney Islands

● Orcadas (Arg)

Falkland
Islands

Sana

Signy (UK)

Georg von Neumayer (FRG)

SOUTH AMERICA

Gen Bernardo O'Higgins (Chile)

Esperanza (Arg)

South Shetland
Islands

Marambio (Arg)

WEDDELL SEA

King George Island

Arturo Prat (Chile)

James Ross Island

Halley (UK) ●

DRAKE PASSAGE

ANTARCTIC
PENINSULA

Palmer (USA)

LARSEN ICE SHELF

Gen Belgrano II (Arg)

Faraday (UK)

Rothera (UK)

GEORGE VI
ICE SHELF

RONNE
ICE SHELF

FILCHNER
ICE SHELF

SOUTH PACIFIC
OCEAN

Gen San Martin (Arg)

Alexander
Island

Dufek M

Pensac
Mount

BELLINGSHAUSEN
SEA

Vinson Massif
Ellsworth
Mountains

90°W

Peter I Øy ○

LESSER
ANTARCTICA

Thurston Island

MARIE BYRD
LAND

59° 00' W

Com Ferraz (Brazil)

King George
Island

AMUNDSEN
SEA

Bellingshausen (USSR)

Artigas (Urug.)

Arctowski (Pol.)

Ten Rodolfo
Marsh (Chile)

Ten Jubany (Arg.)

Siple Island

King Sejong (Korea)

62° 15' S

Great Wall (China)

Russkaya(USSR)

0   5   10   15   20

Kilometres

SOUTHERN OCEAN

0   500   1000   1500   2000

Kilometres